We're All in This Together

quarantined on
The Grand Princess
during COVID-19

MONICA ACHTER

Fulton Books, Inc.
Meadville, PA

Published by Fulton Books 2021

ISBN 978-1-64952-504-8 (paperback)
ISBN 978-1-64952-505-5 (digital)

Printed in the United States of America

INTRODUCTION

Peace be unto thy soul; thine adversity and thine afflictions shall be but a small moment. And then, if thou endure it well, God shall exalt thee on high...

—*Doctrine and Covenants* 121:7–8

Since my experience on the *Grand Princess*, I've had many questions about my trials there. It's difficult to express them in conversation; I needed time to process what happened and find a way of expressing it that would help others understand. That was partially the reason for writing this book. I'm the type to keep emotions deep. I rarely cry in front of others. Throughout the book-writing process, it was cathartic to vent at times and express emotions that I had held inside. This was another reason for writing this book. There will be many accounts of how bad it was being quarantined on a cruise ship during a worldwide pandemic, but I wanted this book to be different.

When I received the letter saying that the *Grand Princess* was in quarantine, my entire world changed. What was once a trip to make lasting memories with aging parents had become one of the most harrowing experiences of my life. My experience on the *Grand Princess* will shape my life for years to come, but not entirely in negative ways. Though there were hardships, there were many lessons learned and many opportunities to test my determination to live the simple law of positivity.

I was under a severe quarantine, away from my family, and under taxing conditions that involved no safe harbor. There were times where it seemed my whole world was collapsing in on me, but with one single moment, I realized I wasn't worried. These questions entered my mind: *Why am I not upset? Why do I think everything is going to be okay?*

The answer was simple: I told myself that everything was going to be okay. Not in the usual dismissive way that optimists often do, but this time, I really felt it. It was more than words; it was conviction. That kind of conviction is born from a lifetime of enduring hardships and realizing that one way or another, they had worked out. After all, I'm still here. This surrender to the moment, knowing that God would provide a way, allowed me a perspective that helped me through one of the most difficult trials of my life.

It wasn't easy. Things didn't magically right themselves, but my perspective changed. Like a child realizing that the monsters in the room are just shadows, tricks of the mind, scattered at the flip of a light switch; I found that the horrible things that seemed so overwhelming before, in this new perspective, were just that—tricks of the mind. I could choose how I viewed my situation, whether I viewed it with an eye of fear or an eye of hope. I chose hope.

My heart goes out to those who lost loved ones on the *Grand Princess*. Their pain far exceeds my own. I also sympathize with those that were traumatized by the experience, who will continue to suffer for years to come. Their suffering is real and should never be dismissed. I hope by telling my own story, I can help others understand your pain.

I've heard many negative comments about how things were handled. There was definitely more than enough bad to focus on. Yet that isn't the only story. When viewed from the right angle, I saw many beautiful things—people coming together in ways that they hadn't before. I saw kindness and sacrifice from complete strangers. I saw faith and conviction. Most of all, I saw God. His hand was there, helping me every step of the way.

My intent in writing this book is to show that there is good in this world. As we find ourselves in the midst of challenging times, I want to invite the world to see things from a different perspective. Look for the light of the positive that leads to good things to come, and reject the fear and hatred that surrounds us. Turn away from that fear in the pit of your stomach and reach out to others without judgment, lending a hand of friendship and charity. This is the only way to move past the trauma toward a more brilliant tomorrow.

I want to look back on my experience not as a grim tragedy but as a token of my belief in the power of being positive and not retreating to the negativity of the world. This book is a documented testimony of that conviction. I hope you will read it with a mind open to the possibility that there is more to life's narrative than the bad news that we are surrounded by. There is real hope in humanity; we just have to choose to see it.

PRINCESS CRUISES

Health Advisory – Coronavirus
March 4, 2020

Dear Princess Guest:

I wish to advise you that we have been notified by the United States Centers for Disease Control and Prevention (CDC) that they are investigating a small cluster of COVID-19 (coronavirus) cases in Northern California connected to a *Grand Princess* voyage that sailed roundtrip San Francisco from February 11 to February 21. We are working closely with our CDC partners and are following their recommendations.

Please be assured that the health, safety, and well-being of all guests and crew are our absolute priority. The CDC is continuing to actively collect information and has set up a meeting with us this morning to determine what, if any, actions need to be taken during this cruise and on arrival in San Francisco. We have shared essential travel and health data with the CDC to facilitate their standard notification to the State and County health authorities to follow up with individuals who may have been exposed to people who became ill.

As we anticipate that further review of the situation will be necessary on arrival in San Francisco, we will be cancelling the call to Ensenada on Thursday, March 5, in order to sail directly to San Francisco and arrive on Thursday afternoon. We will keep you updated with information as we finalize plans. To assist you in contacting your family, we are providing free internet and phone service. We will advise you if the need arises to make changes to your onward travel plans post-cruise.

COVID-19 causes mild illness in about 80% of cases, typically with symptoms of fever, cough and shortness of breath, like the common cold or flu. About 20% of people develop more severe symptoms. The more severe symptoms typically occur in more susceptible individuals that have higher risk factors, such as older adults and those with chronic medical conditions, as it does with regular flu. The illness is mainly spread by droplets from close person-to-person contact. It is possible for the virus to spread by hand touch surfaces, but this is not thought to be the main way the virus spreads. Updated information on the illness can be found at the CDC website: https://www.cdc.gov/coronavirus/2019-ncov/index.html.

As with all respiratory illnesses, particularly during cold and flu season, you can take steps to reduce your risk of illness:
   a. Wash your hands often with soap and water for 20 seconds.
   b. Supplement hand washing by regularly using an alcohol-based hand sanitizer.
   c. Avoid close contact with people suffering from respiratory illness.
   d. Cover your nose and mouth when you cough or sneeze using a tissue or your bent elbow.
   e. Avoid touching your eyes, nose and mouth with unwashed hands.

We are closely recording and monitoring all persons who have reported to the medical center with cold and flu symptoms during the voyage. As a precaution, we are also conducting additional enhanced environmental disinfection onboard in addition to our regular stringent cleaning and sanitation protocols.

If you have experienced any symptoms of acute respiratory illness with fever, chills, or cough at any time during this cruise, and you have not already consulted with the medical staff, please immediately contact the Medical Center by phone to report your illness. There will not be a charge for this service.

Thank you for taking the time to read this important information.

To access complimentary internet, turn on your Wi-Fi and access the "ocean" network for connection.

Yours in health,

[signature]

Grant Tarling, MD, MPH
Chief Medical Officer

AP – A006 - Guest v1.0

CHAPTER 1

The Letter

Wednesday, March 4, 2020
COVID-19.

As my eyes landed on this single word in the letter from the ship's captain, I knew exactly what it meant. I had heard the term before, but in that moment, I didn't realize just how much that word would shape my life during the days that followed on the *Grand Princess* cruise ship. I don't think I fully appreciated the impact it would have. But as my heart sank to my stomach, I instinctively knew that things were about to change. Like how 9/11 shaped the thoughts and feelings of an entire nation, COVID-19 would alter every aspect of life for the entire world. Nothing would be the same.

We were in the last stretch of our Hawaiian cruise and were sailing toward the western coast of Mexico on our way to Ensenada, a small coastal tourist town in Baja California. It was to be the last destination before we disembarked in San Francisco. I had been eagerly waiting to arrive there so I could buy a small souvenir for my grandson. I had promised to get him something since I missed Grandparent's Day at his school.

The cruise was a last-minute thing for me. My parents were invited to go by Quin and Susan, who were some friends of ours from Wyoming, where we built cabins together. Quin and Susan coordinated everything. The whole trip seemed like just the adventure I needed. I felt it might be the last chance I would have to take a trip like this with my parents. My husband's parents were already in an assisted living center and were unable to travel, and I knew the time would come that my parents would be in a similar situation. I didn't want to let this opportunity pass me by. It was also the first time I had been on a cruise, and I was excited to go.

Since the bookings were only for double occupancies, I would have to pay the full-price fare for the room or find someone to share it with me. My husband, Mark, had just started a new job in September and wasn't able to take more time off work as we had just barely gone to Hawaii for two weeks in December. Since I didn't think I could get anyone to come with me on such short notice and I didn't want to pay the full double-occupancy price for a room, I thought this was a sign that maybe I shouldn't go. I had just told my husband that I wasn't going when five minutes later, my mother called, asking me if I would like to stay with Marcie, Quin's little sister, who was traveling alone. The way it all worked out, it was hard not to think that this was meant to be. Within weeks, I was packed and on my way.

One evening just before leaving, my husband and I were watching the news and saw the report on COVID-19 outbreaks on Japanese cruise ships.

"If you get quarantined, I'm not waiting for you," Mark joked.

I glanced at him with a scowl.

"What?" he said defensively. "Who knows how long you'll be in quarantine."

We laughed. At the time, the thought of getting quarantined was so foreign. That could never happen here. Not to us. I was sure the cruise line was taking more precautions now anyway.

Just like the rest of the world, I often lived with the idea that the bad things of the world wouldn't reach us. We are fortunate to live in a country without civil war or strife. Until twenty years ago, the closest we had ever come to having an attack on US soil was Pearl Harbor. The events of 9/11 changed that. Now there is a constant threat of some sort of attack looming over us. I have heard of outbreaks of Ebola in Africa and swine flu and SARS in China and Southeast Asia, but I never considered those things would find their way here. Sure, there were warnings about the next epidemic in the media, but when each year comes and goes with no real impact, how seriously can we take them?

That little exchange between my husband and I seemed harmless at the time. Life, however, has a way of changing perspectives.

The letter came in the night while we slept. It was tucked neatly under our door in the early hours of March 4, day thirteen of the cruise. Marcie found it first, having just woken up to go for coffee with a friend she met on the cruise. As I watched her read the letter, I could tell the news was not good.

"What is it?" I asked. My mind raced, searching for some explanation as to why a letter would be placed under the door in the night. Marcie handed me the letter to read. My greatest concern was that we would not be able to stop at Ensenada. I wouldn't be able to keep my promise to my grandson. But that concern was the last thing on my mind after I read the first sentence.

> *I wish to advise you that we have been notified by the United States Centers for Disease Control and Prevention (CDC) that they are investigating a small cluster of COVID-19 (coronavirus) cases in Northern California connected to a Grand Princess voyage that sailed roundtrip San Francisco...*

I stopped. "What does this mean?"

"It means quarantine."

"It doesn't mention anything about quarantine," I said. "These are just precautionary measures." I continued through the letter.

> *COVID-19 causes mild illness in about 80% of cases, typically symptoms of fever, cough, and shortness of breath, like the common cold or flu. About 20% of people develop more severe symptoms. The more severe symptoms typically occur in more susceptible individuals that have higher risk factors, such as older adults...*

Thoughts of my parents entered my mind along with a flood of desperate worries. I sat down on the bed, bracing myself against the hundreds of questions that swirled through my head. What if they get it? What does it mean, *more severe symptoms*? What kind of symptoms? How many people on the ship have it? How many are going to get it? I had a little bit of a sore throat a couple of days ago; is that a symptom?

Taking a deep breath, I finished reading the letter. There was nothing about passengers having contracted it. I sighed in relief.

"Everything is just precaution," I said reassuringly. "There's nothing to worry about."

I've tried my whole life to be a positive person. I've been through plenty of storms in life, and I have chosen, for better or for worse, to keep a positive outlook. This situation was no different.

I glanced at the pillow sitting next to me.

It read in a large friendly font, *Be Awesome Today*. I brought the pillowcase on the trip because I decided a long time ago not to let my circumstances stop me from being who I knew—and God knew—I could be.

Being positive doesn't mean being blind. I was terrified. But I also knew that the things we're often most afraid of are those things we don't know—the uncertainty of the unknown possibilities that lie ahead.

Fear can be the most destructive power in the world. It fuels hatred and harsh reactions. It justifies our selfishness and insecurities. It keeps us from reaching out and connecting with those around us, especially our loved ones. And if we let it, fear will spread like a small fire across a dry forest and will consume us individually and as a society. I've seen it destroy people, families, and even communities. On one of our port days, I saw firsthand how fear overtook shoppers at the Costco there. People frantically bought out the toilet paper, bottled water, and sanitizing wipes. All over a few media reports. I wasn't about to let that kind of panic take hold in what seemed like an incredibly desperate moment.

I had to keep positive and fight the urge to let my fears dictate my thoughts and actions. No one knew at that time, not even the captain of the ship, what lay in store for us. I decided there was no point of worrying about something that hadn't happened yet.

As I sat there, the memory of taking my children and grandchildren to Disneyland the previous year flashed through my mind. I ached to see them again. Not in my wildest dreams did I think that I would be sitting on a ship in the ocean facing possible quarantine.

What are you going to do now, Monica? I asked myself. The answer came immediately. "I'm going to get breakfast."

An Air of Uncertainty

I decided that I wasn't going to do anything different. I was going to continue to enjoy the trip as if nothing had changed. There were no cases on the ship, and the ship captain and crew were doing everything in their power to make sure no one got infected. There was no reason to doubt that.

With the exception of attendants scrubbing everything with disinfectant, all the services were the same as they had been. The daily activities continued as they did before, and people were still allowed to go about the ship undeterred. It seemed everyone was trying to maintain some semblance of normality in the face of this news. However, despite everyone's best effort to act normal, things had already changed.

It was the quiet that disturbed me the most. People didn't talk to one another like they did before. Although we were mostly strangers aboard the ship, there had been a general friendliness between everyone during the two weeks that we had been together. We had become like family. People would smile and greet you as you passed. Random conversations would spark between unacquainted passengers and crew members. It was one of the more enjoyable parts of the cruise—meeting people from different places and backgrounds. We would swap stories and enjoy the new connections we had formed. This is humanity at its best. But walking to breakfast that morning, the atmosphere was different. Everything seemed somber and foreboding.

No one talked. They went about their activities in a despondent act of will. They ate and played, but not with the same energy they had before. People avoided one another. This was before the concept of social distancing had even formed in the public psyche. We just looked at one another like any of us could be infected. It was like trying to go back to normal after learning there was a murder on the ship and anyone of us could be the killer. There was an air of accusation floating in every interaction.

Was the attendant at the pool infected? What about the couple that we passed in the hall? Was it safe to speak to anyone? We kept our distance while trying to maintain the illusion of normality. In a way, that made the whole thing seem all the more absurd. No one wanted to say it, but we were all afraid. Terror cloaked under a thin smile of politeness. Yet every cough or sneeze that was met with scrutinizing stares revealed the truth. We were all on edge.

My parents got a spot by the pool on the 15th deck, which was the top deck of the pool area. They set up a cluster of loungers away from everyone else for just our family. We spent the day watching a movie and sitting in the sun. Our activities were much like they were before, but they felt different. Before, we were involved in them. They were done for the pure enjoyment they brought. Now everything felt stale and lifeless. We were just going through the motions in order to distract ourselves from thinking about the letter and what was going to happen to us. It passed the time, and that was all.

My phone went off. I checked the caller ID, wondering if it was my husband again. I had already spoken to him that morning to tell him about the letter. I was encouraging on the call and told him there was nothing to be worried about. He was anxious enough just having me on a cruise without him. He has had issues in the past with abandonment that he learned to deal with through counseling. This was the first time that I had taken an extended trip without him. He was supportive, but I knew it was hard for him.

The caller ID showed that it was Ashley, a friend of mine who worked at the local news channel back home. I answered.

"Monica," the voice on the other end announced.

"Ashley," I exclaimed. "How are you doing?"

"I should be asking you that," she replied. "Is everything okay? Your husband called me and told me that you are on the *Grand Princess*. That they were worried about an outbreak of COVID-19."

"Everything is fine," I said, reassuring her. I wasn't about to succumb to hysteria now. *Positivity to the end*, I thought to myself. I had to be brave; I had to stay strong. I didn't want to worry anyone at home, and I certainly didn't want to be a burden.

"Have they told you anything?" she asked. "Is anyone on the ship infected?" Although Ashley was a reporter, she was a friend first. I knew these questions were out of concern for me rather than the beginnings of an interview.

"They are just taking precautions," I replied. I didn't want to alarm the world with a bunch of speculation that I knew nothing about. "There are no reported cases. Everything is business as usual. I'm not worried a bit."

"Your husband seemed pretty worried," Ashley said, unconvinced by my lack of concern.

"You know Mark," I said. "He was worried the day I stepped on this boat."

She laughed. "I know this may not be the most opportune time," said Ashley, "but I thought maybe we could do an interview over FaceTime."

"Well, it would take away from my vacation." There was a pause. "I'm joking. Of course, we can do an interview."

I spent the next few hours taking Ashley on a FaceTime tour of the ship. My intention was to assure people back home that there was nothing to worry about. I wanted to keep things positive. At the time, I didn't know anything outside of the letter, which said nothing of the number of potential cases or the specifics of what had caused the reaction from the cruise line.

Unknownst to me at the time, there were three passengers who had sailed on the ship prior to our cruise that were known to have contracted COVID-19. One of them, a seventy-one-year-old man, died that very day that we received the letter. There were, at the time, 11 passengers and 10 crew members who showed potential symptoms of COVID-19. The *Grand Princess*, our cruise ship—with 2,422 guests and 1,111 crew members from 23 nations—was reported to be on its way to San Francisco for docking. And discussions were already underway as to whether we should be allowed to dock at all.

Had I known that information at the time, I hope that I would have been just as positive. I also would hope that had I known how I would be tested over the next few weeks in quarantine, I would have maintained that same positivity. But we don't get a crystal ball. We don't see what lies ahead. I like to think that our inability to see the future can be a gift. Though it can often breed fear, it can also give rise to hope. It is up to us which of these seeds we decide to cultivate in the uncertainties of our hearts.

The CDC Arrive

Marcie and I were sitting on our beds chatting online when the silence was interrupted by an announcement over the room intercom. There was normally nothing unusual about these announcements. They took place throughout the day during the trip. Most were about special activities that people could participate in. Now they were a means to keep us updated on anything concerning our predicament. The worst part of being stuck in the cabins was not knowing what was going on outside. The announcement was a way of alleviating that uncertainty, though sometimes it just led to more questions.

"This is the bridge. A helicopter operation is about to take place. During this operation, the open decks will be closed to all persons not involved with the operation."

There was no information at that time of who was on the helicopter or why it was there. Obviously, something serious was happening, or they wouldn't have had us stay in the cabins. Maybe they were just being cautious. At this point, no one had been tested aboard the ship, so there was no indication that anyone was even infected.

We were told not to go outside the room, and if anyone came to the door, we were to put on a mask. They set up a line that we could call if we needed anything. Although we were not supposed to leave our rooms, we often looked out our door to see if there was any activity going on. Sometimes we could hear talking or movement outside. At times, an attendant would be there and would caution us to keep the doors closed. Other times, the hall would be completely empty.

On one occasion as I looked out the door, I saw medical workers dressed in personal protective equipment. They were carrying a red bag with a biohazard symbol printed on the side. I assumed these were the people who came on the helicopter, likely from the CDC. The captain did say there would be testing, but we had thought it would not be until we docked. They must have sent the helicopter in anticipation of our docking in San Francisco. Again, in my mind, these were all precautionary measures. They meant nothing at the time.

Ye Shall Not Fear

That evening, I was alone in my room. Marcie was out visiting other people. She often went to visit her brother, who was also on the cruise ship. She and I seemed to hit it off right away and quickly become friends, but because we began the trip as strangers, when things got more serious, I think she needed someone that she could confide in. So she spent a lot of time away. During that time,

I thought of what I should do next, trying to anticipate what might happen. It was, of course, impossible to know what lay ahead. It was so far outside the normal for anyone. Still, the process of making a plan helped me.

I thought that we might end up spending a lot of time in our room. I decided that if that were true, I was going to need some major distractions. I went to the library and grabbed Trivial Pursuit, Scattergories, and a deck of cards. I then decided that I would get up early the next day to do my laundry. I had enough clothes to last the trip, but I thought that if we were delayed, I should be prepared. I had no real reason to suspect that we would be detained or that we would be locked in our room. At the time, they were just scenarios playing out in my head. Rather than worry about them, I found solutions to them. It was like my way of coping with the uncertainty of the situation. There is a verse of scripture that I often think of that might explain my mind-set: "If ye are prepared, ye shall not fear."

When approaching the lion's mouth, it's impossible not to be afraid. However, if you are prepared with a nice T-bone to offer the lion, it's not nearly as scary. At the time, I had no influence on the decisions of politicians. I couldn't stop the spread of COVID-19 on the ship. And I certainly had no control of the passengers and their reactions to a possible outbreak. But with the games, I now had something to ease my time in my cabin. And the next day, I would make sure that I had clean clothes.

In the pile of clothes was the dress that I had worn to the ship's first formal dinner. It was a traditional island dress that had belonged to my grandmother who wore it fifty years prior on a trip to Hawaii. It was purple with a fuschia floral print. My grandfather had a matching shirt, but my dad had told me it was given to the secondhand store. When the night of the formal dinner came, my father came to my room wearing the shirt. He had kept it after all.

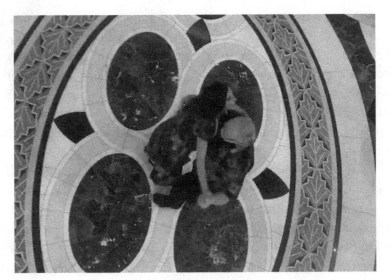

Father daughter dance

My grandparents wearing the Hawaiian clothes 50 years ago

After dinner, we went to the large open piazza area on one of the mid-decks. There was dancing with traditional island music. At one point in the night, my father and I danced together—me in my grandmother's dress, and he in my grandfather's shirt. It was like the two were reunited once more. That night was the highlight of my trip. It was the whole reason I came, to have a wonderful opportunity to make beautiful memories with my parents. I will forever treasure that moment.

I sighed as I gathered the dress and the rest of the laundry. This was not what I had in mind for a trip with my parents. I reached into my luggage and pulled out the Tide pods and fabric softener that I packed in case of an emergency. Mark would have laughed at me packing detergent on a cruise. "When are you going to have time to do laundry?" he would have said. My heart ached thinking of Mark. How long would it be before I would see him again? I held the detergent and softener tightly against my chest as tears welled in my eyes. I wished Mark was with me. The emergency was upon me now. There was nothing I could do to stop it. But if I had to face it, I was going to go into it prepared. It wasn't much, but it was enough to keep the fear at bay so I could sleep that night.

CHAPTER 2

A Change in the Air

Thursday, March 5, 2020
Day one of quarantine and day fourteen of the cruise.

When I woke up the next morning, despite all the unknowns, I felt a little more hopeful. I looked at the words on my pillow and decided I was going to face the day with a cheerful heart. I woke up early to wash my clothes at the onboard Laundromat. There was no one there; maybe because it was early or maybe they just didn't feel they needed it. After all, we thought we would be docking in San Francisco soon, and I imagine doing laundry seemed pointless to many. But somehow, I overwhelmingly felt I needed to do it.

As I folded the last of my laundry and placed it in the basket, I was reminded of the last time I saw my husband before boarding the plane at the airport. I had packed everything the night before so I would be ready to go the next morning. I didn't like rushing; perhaps it's part of the need to be prepared. To conserve space in my luggage, I had gotten in the habit of stuffing extra clothes into a neck pillow that I took on the plane. It worked well for me in the past, so I did the same this time. In my rush to the airport terminal, I forgot my neck pillow in the car, and Mark had already pulled away and was heading into work. This was not a good way to start out my trip.

I didn't realize my mistake until I arrived at the terminal, and I couldn't go back for it without missing the plane. Luckily, my wonderful husband was willing to turn around and bring it to me. It made him late for work, which may have put a damper on his day.

But it did allow me one more chance to see him before I left. In light of everything that had happened since that moment and the possibilities that lay ahead, I cherished that extra time. And of course, one more kiss.

At breakfast, we weren't allowed to dish up our own food. It was like we were helpless children needing someone to get our food for us. We were told that these were precautionary measures recommended by the CDC. The ship attendants didn't seem as accommodating as they were before. They herded us into lines and were gruff with us if we didn't follow the established procedure. It was as if they blamed us for bringing the virus aboard. I imagine they were under intense pressure because of the circumstances we were in, which may have caused them to buckle a bit under that pressure.

We were all on edge. I struggled to be social. There was a family with five children standing behind me in line. The mother was friendly and talkative. She spoke of her toddler who had a fever a couple of days prior. I was concerned for her, but she assured me her baby was all better. I didn't feel that I was going to contract the virus. The possibility of quarantine lingering over my head was more threatening than the virus. I was cordial in listening to her. I could tell though that others in line were uncomfortable with the conversation. I was surprised how attitudes had changed in such a short time. A conversation that was perfectly ordinary the day before now produced an unsettling feeling.

I got my food and sat alone at a table next to a window overlooking the ocean. I have always loved the ocean. As I sat there, an older couple wandered around looking for a place to sit. The husband approached my table and asked, "May we sit here?"

"Of course," I replied, offering them the seats across from me.

We talked while we ate. They were a cute couple. They reminded me of my own parents. As I listened to their story, I reflected on how difficult the whole situation must have been for them. I had heard that the virus was most dangerous to the elderly and those with other health conditions. I considered myself pretty healthy and didn't worry about my body's ability to fight off the disease. Perhaps that was reassurance from God or lack of understanding of just how serious COVID-19 was. My main concern was my parents. How well would they be able to handle the virus? I tried to brush the thought aside. But it continued to plague me.

After breakfast, I made my way to the internet cafe with my mom. Cruise ships often provide internet to patrons, accessible through Wi-Fi. It's often costly, and I didn't feel I would need it on the trip. However, given the concerning situation, the cruise line opened the internet up to everyone at no cost. In order to benefit from this, you had to sign up at the internet cafe. By the time we arrived, the line was already extremely long. Marcie had purchased the internet the day we boarded the ship, so she waited while Quin, Susan, my mom, and I stood in line.

It was already evident, waiting in that line, that tensions were increasing among the passengers. For the most part, it was guised under polite conversations and strained smiles. But there was definitely something insincere about it, evidenced when a woman just behind us started coughing. Suddenly, the conversations stopped, and a hush fell on the passengers as they turned to stare.

It was more than just an awkward silence that was disturbing. It was the fear in the eyes of the passengers as they watched the woman coughing that was disconcerting. It may have just been a coughing fit brought on by some water going down the wrong tube or from breathing in the same dry recirculated air. We were all on the verge of a cough at any given moment. But to everyone looking, it was a reminder of the plague that threatened us all. She might as well have been an untouchable leper.

The coughing settled, and the woman regained her composure. She scanned the crowd, realizing how this seemingly innocent act must look to them. Putting a hand up as if to quell their anxiety, she exclaimed, "I'm okay. I'm not sick." She smiled disarmingly at everyone watching.

There was a slight chuckle from the group of onlookers, but even this seemed forced. The truth was, nobody knew who was sick and who wasn't. Was a cough just a simple irritation in the throat or something more? It had been a day since receiving the letter, and already suspicions were circulating. Things like a cough or a sneeze that were once dismissed were now scrutinized. Conversations of a sick family member, which meant nothing before, became uncomfortable and almost taboo.

After signing up for the internet, my mother left to find my father. I took the opportunity to go to the top deck for some exercise. I don't know why we all decided to go off and do our own things. I guess we just needed some time alone to process things, to figure things out. I went to the hot tub to do water aerobics. I thought that if we were quarantined, I wouldn't get another chance to exercise. It also helped to alleviate the stress of everything going on. It was therapeutic.

I had been through hard things before. There were times during my husband's fight against prescription-drug addiction that I thought I couldn't go on. It was a difficult time for us all, but we got through with a saying that we held dear: "I can do hard things." Now my husband is an example to me as he helps counsel others struggling through addiction. "I can do hard things" has now become a motto for my husband and me. It is a reminder to us that no matter the hardship, we can endure, and at the end of it, there is always something greater.

When Susan and I were whale watching on a small boat off the coast of Maui, she was nervous about being on the boat. I told her the same thing. "We can do hard things." Now I was repeating the words to myself as I reflected on what was happening. It helped put things in perspective. I took the time while I was alone to make a game plan to try to anticipate different scenarios. With a plan, things always seemed more manageable, even if things didn't turn out the way I wanted. The simple act of creating a plan gave me hope and helped me feel like I had some control in an otherwise powerless situation. The plan could be as simple as determining to make my bed each day in quarantine. One could argue that this does not solve the problem, but not all problems are meant to be solved. Some are just meant to be endured.

Endurance takes a different kind of planning than the usual problem-solution approach. The only way to endure a seemingly hopeless situation is to find ways to foster hope in yourself. If making the bed each day convinces you that the world isn't going to end, then do it. It's not a lie, and it's not useless because it gets you through and keeps you from giving up. Most of the problems in life are out of our control or require a persistent effort that lasts weeks, months, or even years. Problems like these demand the willpower to continue.

There was nothing I could do to prevent what was coming, and there was no solution in sight. That is a difficult place to be—an uncertain future with no control over the outcome. My only choice was in how I would react. I decided it is what it is, and the only way out was through. I just wanted to make sure that my actions getting through this trial reflected the person I knew I was. I had to stay positive and not give in to fear.

Around noon, I joined my parents and the rest of the group for lunch. Little did we know this would be our last meal together on the ship. They had already announced that all activities were canceled for the day, but shortly after lunch, they requested everyone to go back to their rooms. The lockdown had begun.

Our last meal together before we quarantined

Quarantine

Our room had a living space of about ten feet by eleven feet. Including the bathroom, it was 160 square feet total. There were two beds where Marcie and I slept, which took up a substantial portion of the space. There were mirrors on opposite walls to give the illusion that the room was bigger than it actually was. However, when locked in the room for days at a time, the small dimensions of the room become quite apparent. Since ours was an interior cabin, we had no balcony or window to get fresh air, and the only lighting was artificial from lamps. The air was stale, the quarters cramped, and we had no idea how long we would be confined in such a small space.

Our inside cabin

I've always had claustrophobia. I believe this came from an incident as an infant where I managed to cover my face in a plastic bag, nearly suffocating myself. My mother said I was totally blue. I don't know if things like that can have a lasting impact on our psyche, but sitting in that room, facing the idea that I would have to spend the immediate future between those four paneled walls, the anxiety set in.

The ship attendants brought around menus and forms to fill out. Most of it was information about our travel and our intended destination after the cruise. They also had forms to request medications that would be needed in the event that we were delayed. At that point, we were under the impression that we would be ending our trip early. We made our order and put the time in for 6:00 p.m. Sliding the menus under the door along with the forms, we went back to chatting with our family. Marcie had set up a group text with everyone that was on the ship. It was good to have that contact, especially since my parents were down another hall and we were not allowed to leave the room.

Marcie and I talked about the situation, but I don't think either of us had a real understanding of what was happening and what the future held. I could tell that she was having a tough time like me, but she tried not to show it. I didn't expect that she would. It was difficult to really open up with each other because we had only just met on this trip. Her real confidant was her brother and his wife, but they were in another cabin. So she and I spent a lot of time on our phones chatting with family and friends.

The captain added extra movies and channels to help with passing the time. I had seen most of the shows, but Marcie was not as much of a moviegoer; so we watched some of the shows she hadn't seen. She would lay on her belly on the bed with her head cradled in her hands, watching the TV. I would usually half watch and half look at my phone.

I didn't mind though. Like I said, I had already seen the movies and wasn't paying attention that much anyway. I was just glad to have another person in the room. I can't imagine having to be faced with this lockdown alone. I know that I could talk to people over the phone or chat, but it's a different feel having a person there talking to you. There's a feeling of connection—an energy of sorts that doesn't exist through a digital medium.

I had the games that I picked up the night before, but we didn't play them. With everything going on, we weren't much into playing games. I played solitaire with the cards, but after hearing a news report that COVID-19 could stay on surfaces for several days, the thought of touching the cards became unsettling. What if the last person who used them had the virus? I didn't want to risk exposure, especially with the CDC testing people on the ship. I just wanted the ship to dock so I could be cleared and go home.

The Blame Game

I had a few more phone calls from my friend, Ashley, and other journalists, asking questions about what was going on. Unfortunately, I didn't have answers, and I didn't want to speculate. Marcie didn't think I should be taking interviews in the first place. She felt that the ship's captain or someone who knew something should be taking the interviews. I didn't necessarily disagree with her, but I felt the journalists just wanted to get a human angle. I was going through the event, and they wanted to hear what it was like.

I'm not the type to exaggerate the situation, and I always tried to keep it positive. On several occasions, the interviewer tried to get me to give the whole thing a negative spin. I suppose that sort of thing sells bigger in the news, but I didn't give in. I had already decided to stay positive. And up to that point, other than being held in my room for a day, I really had nothing to complain about.

There were some on board who did complain rather vocally. We could hear them outside the door complaining to the ship attendants. Especially that night when dinner was late. Our dinner was supposed to arrive at 6:00 p.m. but didn't come until 10:30 p.m. We were hungry and tired, but we felt that there was no point standing at the door yelling at the attendants. They were probably tired and hungry too. I'm sure they were doing the best they could, given the situation they were in. We had no idea what they were going through. Maybe it wasn't their fault. Maybe the CDC was testing them and they couldn't get dinner started soon enough. Maybe they were shorthanded because other crew members were sick. And maybe they just didn't anticipate how long it would take to deliver meals to over three thousand people across the ship.

Blame is a terrible thing. For many, our first impulse when something bad happens is to find someone to blame. But blame isn't always simple. It's not always easy to see who's at fault. And sometimes those individuals who are responsible are never found.

Perhaps one day, we'll have all the facts about COVID-19 and know exactly how it started. But at the time, all we had was speculative blame being thrown around. This isn't helpful. It doesn't solve the immediate threat. I agree that justice should be served if there was ill intent or that corrections should be made if it was a result of negligence. But that can be taken care of after the crisis has passed. All it does during a crisis is sow seeds of contention that make the problem worse.

I couldn't imagine the cruise line would intentionally spread a virus aboard their ship, and there was no evidence of negligence. There were probably things that could have been done differently, but it's easier to see that looking back. No one on that cruise ship could have anticipated a virus like COVID-19. I do know that the crew worked long, arduous hours trying to take care of the passengers in a less-than-ideal situation. Sure, some could have been more kind, but they were all under stress. They were going through the same things we were, but they had to keep working while their fellow crew members fell victim to the virus. I'm sure the thought lingered heavily on their minds that they might become infected too, yet they continued to do their job.

It's difficult to be on the front line of a crisis—whether you're a nurse, a police officer, a soldier, or even a convenience-store clerk. We are human, and we don't always handle stress well. Those who step up and stand the line between order and chaos should be commended, whether we completely agree with their actions in the moment or not.

I may never know why dinner was late that night, but that was the least of our worries. Trying to lay the blame on some poor, tired attendant wasn't going to solve anything. It was a bad situation all around. Blame only serves to create division and increases tensions on already worn nerves.

The Deciding Moment

Mornings were hard when isolated in a room with no windows. There was no way to acclimate to the day. The only indication of time was the clock on our phones. I went about my morning as usual, though there was no anticipation of activities or events other than sitting in the cabin, whittling away our day on the phone. My husband had to work, so I wouldn't be able to FaceTime with him until he got off work. That was the real highlight for the day. Given that I had received several phone calls by journalists the day before, it seemed likely that I would have more.

The morning silence was broken by the sound of my phone. It was Ashley.

"Hey, Ashley," I answered. "Is everything okay?"

"Have you heard the news?" she asked. Her voice was frantic.

"No. What news?"

There was a pause. Then Ashley's stifled voice. "They found confirmed cases of COVID-19 on the ship."

With those words, my worst fears were realized. What had once been just precautionary measures were now a real threat. If there was even just one, we would be quarantined for two weeks. How long would it be before it spread to the whole ship—if it hadn't already?

I did not speak for some time. I didn't know what to think, let alone what to say. I had heard that only 20 percent show symptoms. I didn't feel sick. I just saw my parents yesterday, and they seemed fine. Maybe we haven't been infected. My desperate attempt at staying calm was like putting a hand against a tsunami, expecting it to stop.

"I'm sure everything is going to be fine," said Ashley reassuringly. "They haven't announced anything yet."

"Thank you for letting me know," I said. "I should probably tell the others."

"There's nothing to worry about," she said. "You've got this."

I nodded as I placed the phone down. *I've got this*, I repeated in my head. My body felt heavy and weak. As I sat there questioning how we would weather this storm, I was reminded of the storm we faced as we set sail from the island of Hilo.

It was a fierce storm that swept in from the south, blanketing the skies with menacing clouds and torrential rain. I had never been in a storm aboard a ship before. The sea was in turmoil. Waves thrashed at the side of the ship that bobbed back and forth, rising with each swell and falling again and again. Although the large scale of the ship helped to lessen the motion, it was still unsettling, especially during the rougher parts. There were several rooms on several decks that had the storm water come in and flood them.

For the next two days, the storm followed us across the Pacific, and the buffeting continued. During this time, there were some passengers that chose to stay in their cabins because it was too hard to walk around the rocking ship. As I made my way to the buffet area, I could see people struggling to dish up plates. Several times during some of the bigger swells, someone would be tossed around so hard that they would drop their plates. I asked a crewman, Guido, if this kind of storm was normal.

"This is the worst I've seen it," he replied. "At least without the captain changing course."

I remember heading to the customer service desk on the sixth deck to see the status of the waves. A monitor displayed information about the ship and the current conditions of the storm. The swells had increased to nine meters, which is about thirty feet. The swells were so big that the lower outside deck had to be closed and parts of the upper decks as well, and the water in the pools was thrown beyond their walls, spilling over the deck and out to sea. Eventually, the pools had to be drained of water. With each movement, the ship creaked as if ready to snap. To prevent us from rolling over onto our side, the captain deployed the ship's stabilizers, fins that extend out the hull of the ship similar to the shape of airplane wings. As the water flows over the stabilizers, it can be turned upward or downward to exert dive or lift but does nothing to prevent pitching from the front of the ship to the aft or rear.

The empty pool

The whole experience was frightening and a little adventurous, but still there was confidence that we would make it through. We trusted that the captain knew what he was doing and that the ship could withstand the storm. After all, the ships were built for this, and the captain was well trained and experienced.

At the time of that storm, we had no idea what lay ahead of us. No one suspected that an even bigger storm was brewing. Yet the emotional tides I faced knowing there was COVID on our ship was every bit as real as those waves that crashed against the ship. Little did I know that in the days that lie ahead, I would rise and fall many times with the swells of emotion and discouragement. The question I faced was, would I break against the waves or weather the storm to the end?

I looked back at the words scrawled across my pillow. *Be Awesome Today.* Somehow I didn't feel quite as awesome as I did the day before. The choice lay in front of me, suspended between conflicting thoughts. Do I choose fear, or do I choose hope? Sometimes that choice is more difficult to make, especially in the midst of a storm. At that moment, it seemed impossible. It would take strength beyond my own to get through this.

During the more frightening times of the storm that struck the ship at sea, I sang the hymn "Peace Be Still." It was a reminder to me that I wasn't alone and that God could not only calm the physical storms of life, but He could calm the storms that rage within us all. My heart groaned a silent prayer to God. *I can't do this alone.* Without hesitation, the response came: *We've got this.*

Me and Marcie

CHAPTER 3

The Little Things

Friday, March 6–Saturday, March 7, 2020
Day two and three of quarantine and day fifteen and sixteen of the cruise.

It's the little things you miss when stuck in quarantine. Spending two days in a cramped room with no windows helps you appreciate the little things that are often taken for granted. Being able to walk up and down the stairs. Feeling the breeze on my face. Smelling the fresh clean air. Basking in the glow of the sun. Vitamin D. My health has always been important to me, and I have always made exercise a part of my routine. At home, I would go to a water-aerobics class every morning at the local swimming pool. Physical exercise was just a small portion of my routine. The social part of my workout did more to increase my endorphins than the exercises. A cramped compartment was not the ideal workout room. It felt strange and confining.

Along with the cramped quarters, each day that passed in the compartment, the air got more stale, and the room more confining. And as my energy level decreased, it became harder to get out of bed. My body felt heavy, being weighed down by the uncertainty of this new trial. I craved fresh air to breathe and the sun warming my face. I needed to get out of the cabin. Since smoking was not allowed in the cabins, the captain had arranged for smokers to be taken to the upper decks to smoke. I have to admit that this seemed cruelly unfair. After all, they were just going up there to inhale a cigarette. They wouldn't even appreciate the fresh air. Marcie joked that maybe it was time to take up smoking.

I knew the effects of addictions like drugs and cigarettes from my experiences with my husband's addictions. So I recognized that their need for that smoke was probably far more than my need for fresh air. Still, I desired more than anything to leave the cabin. At times, I would find myself pacing from the bed to the door, looking through the peephole and back to the bed. Anxiety would then set in. When that happened, I would take a deep breath and find a distraction. When the captain finally announced that they were trying to get permission to give passengers time on the top deck, I let out a scream and almost leapt for joy, although leaping was nearly impossible in our confined quarters.

Going on the top deck meant that not only would I get that sun and fresh air I was starving for but I would also see my parents and life would feel normal again. Although we were just down the hall from each other, they may as well have been across the ocean. Under orders from the CDC, we were not allowed to leave our rooms to visit others on the ship. That's not to say it didn't happen, but I struggle going against rules—even when those rules seem completely unnecessary.

Sure, we talked and chatted on the phone, but it wasn't the same as having them there in front of me. I was definitely a daddy's girl and felt it comforting to have him hug me and tell me it's going to be all right. I was also concerned about their health. I knew that if they were getting sick, they would probably try to hide it from me. They're the type of people who don't like to make a fuss and put people out. Even I would try to hide a small cough for fear that others might think I was getting sick. Any sign of the sickness could mean a lengthy quarantine.

My mother has diabetes and needs to eat regularly. But with the chaos of trying to organize food deliveries every day, meals often came irregularly and were not at all what she needed. Meals were mostly made up of leftover dinner rolls, so hard they would tear up the roof of your mouth. My parents tried several times to reach customer service to order diabetic food and medicine on the ship's phone, but it would just ring endlessly. So they gave up.

I guess God knew I needed that little bit of reassurance that my parents were being taken care of because I managed to create a good rapport with the steward on our deck, and I would ask him to take some healthy snacks and refreshments to my parents' cabin. Not all stewards were as friendly or accommodating as that steward. He was very obliging, something I will forever be thankful for and will always remember. As far as I am concerned, those like that steward will be lifelong friends.

Waiting for the opportunity to go to the top deck, I felt like a child waiting for Santa Claus to deliver Christmas presents. Knowing that it might be possible for me to go up on the deck to feel the glorious sun on my skin, breathe in the fresh air, and hug my sweet parents gave me something to hope for. It seems like such a small thing, but at the time, it meant everything. The captain was exceptionally good about trying to give us something to hope for. He couldn't offer much, but what he did offer helped us more than he could ever know.

Finding Solutions Instead of Problems

One of the most difficult emotions to manage in the situation we found ourselves in was the feeling of being powerless. I desperately tried to find little things that I could do in order to retain some semblance of control over my life. Even the small act of getting dressed in the morning was at least something. But these small gestures only put off the feeling for a time. As it is with the majority of people in similar circumstances, the mind eventually sees through the ploy, and the depression sets in. What's the point in getting up, getting showered, getting dressed, and putting on makeup to go nowhere? There had to be something more meaningful that I could do—something that I genuinely believed would make a difference in our situation. I needed a purpose. That purpose came from two unexpected experiences: an e-mail that Marcie received and the inspired leadership of the ship's captain.

Marcie's e-mail was a message from the governor of Nevada addressed to Marcie herself. He had sent the e-mail to let her know that he was doing everything in his power to make sure she returned home quickly and safely. I don't know how sincere he was; maybe it was just one of those letters that politicians send to keep their constituents happy. But the fact was, he didn't have to send it, and it was sincere enough to give us some hope. He was someone in a powerful position that might have sway. Having him recognize our plight and being willing to use his power to help gave us reassurance. I wondered if our governor was doing the same thing. I had to find out.

The captain of the ship acted in the same way. His announcements were always reassuring and designed to give us something to hope for. Does that mean that everything worked out the way he intended or that there weren't things that he did not tell us? Of course not. I'm sure there were many things he would have liked to tell us, but he either did not have permission or simply did not know himself. There were things that were out of his control. Still, he made sure we felt that reassurance that things were going according to a plan and would eventually work out. We have a saying, "Everything works out for Marcie." Likewise, everything works out for me too!

On one occasion, Susan and Quin overheard Captain John Smith through the wall speaking to the crew. The walls of the cabin were thin, and it was easy to hear what was going on in the hall and other rooms. Somewhere, though I can't be sure where, the captain was meeting with the crew. First, she could vaguely make out the conversation, but then she had the idea of putting a glass against the wall to hear better.

"What are they saying?" Quin asked. They were like two schoolkids trying to snag the latest gossip. I guess when you're stuck in a room with no outlet, you do some crazy things.

Susan hushed him and strained to listen. "It's the captain," she whispered.

"What's he saying?" he asked. He was eager to hear anything new. When would we dock? How long would we be locked in our cabins? Would we be able to go back home?

She waved her hand, signaling for him to stop talking. Sitting with her ear pressed against the glass, she listened intently. He waited, hoping to hear something that would feed his curiosities and maybe comfort his uncertainties.

"He's talking to the crew," she said.

"What about?" he asked. "Are we going to be docking soon?"

"Shhh." She smacked him on the arm. "I'm trying to listen."

A few moments passed before she started recounting what she heard, like a translator translating some unheard language. "He is telling them how much he appreciates how they are handling the situation," she whispered. "He says they are doing a really good job taking care of the passengers."

"He's giving them a pep talk?" he asked.

Susan nodded while continuing to listen. "He's asking, 'Who are we?'" She paused. "Now they are all yelling back, *'Grand Princess!'*"

"*Who are we?*"

"*Grand Princess!*"

"*Who are we?*"

"*Grand Princess!*"

The chant repeated louder and louder until it could be heard through the wall without the glass. The captain ended with one sentence that stuck with me: "We're all in this together."

While it was disappointing that we didn't get any of the juicy news that we wanted, it was still very touching. And our hearts were softened toward such a wonderful captain and crew. The captain was proud of his ship and crew and, like any good leader would, was trying to keep their morale up in an otherwise discouraging situation. He didn't have the power to change the situation, but he used his power to do what he could. He gave the crew and passengers as much hope as he could. He stayed positive, not because he knew how things were going to work out but because he probably understood that there was no point in giving into fears. It serves no one.

It seemed the captain had made the same choice that I had that first day, and it made all the difference. I doubt he handled things perfectly, and I'm sure mistakes were made. But the fact that he chose to stay positive and refused to give in to his fears went a long way in helping the passengers and crew through an extremely difficult situation. That's good leadership.

In the end, we're all captains of our own ship, each trying to make our way through the storms of life. How we decide to conduct that ship matters. What thoughts we entertain, what we do with the limited powers we have—they all matter. And they will determine whether we make it safely through the storm or we figuratively sink into the depths of despair.

I decided that I would conduct myself in the same way that the captain did. I would do everything in my power to help the situation and not give in to my fears. I would stay positive and look for solutions rather than gripe about the problems. The e-mail from Marcie's governor inspired me to reach out to my own government representatives. I called, e-mailed, and texted anyone I could. I even got responses from some, including Congressman Ben McAdams. He technically wasn't from our district, but he wanted to do all he could to help us out. While he was in Washington fighting for us, he contracted the virus himself and ended up in the hospital fighting for his life. Also Lt. Governor Spencer Cox and his team for the countless hours they spent on our behalf. We will forever be in their debt for their efforts.

I contacted Mark and gave him all the phone numbers and contact information I had received from friends and reporters. He then set to work and put the wheels in motion from the home-front side. He even involved our oldest son to contact officials through Twitter, and friends and family members were putting out the word through Facebook also. Through the whole ordeal, prayers were being constantly said on our behalf.

I don't know if our simple communications had any sway on our situation, but they were at least something. They helped me feel that we were doing everything within our power. I also started to give myself my own little pep talks. Little things like complimenting how I handled myself in a particular situation or giving myself encouragement that things would get better. This eventually spilled over to others, whether it was thanking the steward for his service or giving Marcie an encouraging word.

These efforts are simple and subtle. They can be easily dismissed by the naysayer. But it's these little acts that get us through some of the hardest trials in life. I am living proof of that. These simple acts of kindness made all the difference for me and gave me something to look forward to. Spreading goodness is more contagious than any virus will ever be.

Tender Mercies

Early Sunday morning. I opened the cabin door to find face masks hanging from the door handles. I could see them all up and down the hallway; every door had them. The cruise line gave permission for passengers to go to the top deck. I thought I might burst with anticipation. I imagined the feel of the sun on my face and the smell of the ocean spray. I thought of my parents and being able to see them and hug them again for what could be the very last time. Something that just days ago I took for granted was now the sweetest gift.

They started with the lower decks and slowly worked their way up deck by deck. The inside cabins were given precedence since the outer cabins had balconies, which gave them access to fresh air and sunlight. They started in the morning and continued throughout the day. The hours passed slowly as we waited. Once the afternoon arrived and they were still several decks away from ours, it became apparent that our day in the sun would not come.

The time for getting each deck to the top deck, allowing them to walk around and get them back to their cabins, took much longer than anticipated. We kept opening the door to see if people were going anywhere. The neighbor across the hall did too. We would talk, and she told us the people in the outside rooms, the cabins with balconies, had all decided to give up their time up top so all of us with interior cabins could get out. That was such an amazing gesture and brought tears to our eyes and touched our hearts deeply.

Despite the crew's best effort, they would not be able to get through all the decks. Since our deck was toward the end of the list, we would not be able to make it before the sun went down. What started out bringing such hope and joy slowly whittled down to despair. It's hard to move forward when hopes are crushed. It seems like such a small thing now, but that trip to the top deck was something I desperately held on to and hoped for. It's what got me through another day, and then it was gone. There was a sense of betrayal, as if hope itself betrayed me.

Some people may wonder why I invest so much in things to hope for. Especially given the fact that if I didn't hope at all, I would never have to be disappointed. But it's a natural part of life that things don't always work out the way we want them to. Expectations minus results equals frustrations. Sometimes the naysayers and skeptics are right, and things do go wrong. But that doesn't mean we should give up and hope for nothing. There's nothing gained by giving up hope and applying skepticism instead. Both the hopeful and the hopeless are in the same predicament. The only difference is that those who are hopeless started their despair early, while those who maintained hope had a few more moments of joy.

I don't think there's any eternal bet between the skeptics and the believers over who's right and who's wrong most often. Sometimes the hopeful believers are wrong when they say things are going to work out and then they don't. Other times, the skeptics are proven wrong by a determined believer who accomplishes the impossible. In the end, the hopeful heart brings greater joy and possibilities than the skeptic that brings nothing. For that reason alone, hope should be embraced by everyone.

While it's true that sometimes hoping for something may bring you disappointment, moments of disappointment are a small price to pay for a lifetime of joy. This is why I will choose hope every single time. Often what looks like the end of hope is merely the beginning of a greater hope.

The captain came over the intercom again saying it was dinnertime and they would stop taking people out for air for the day. We were crushed! We wanted to cry. As I sat faced with despair for the loss of something I hoped for, a knock came at the door. It was Darla staying in the room across the hallway. She had knocked and quickly ran back to her room and waited for us with her door still ajar.

Darla's room across the hall

She pressed her mask against her face and, in a muffled voice, said, "Sorry to bother you, but I was wondering if you would like to come over and step out on the balcony of my room." Confused, we looked down the hall for the attendant, expecting him to come and tell us to go back inside. Seeing our confusion, she added, "Don't worry, no one's looking."

Since the cabins are so small, we could see all the way across her room to her balcony. Her sliding glass door was open, and we could see the ocean and the beautiful sunset. Just then, a breeze came rushing in and across our faces; with tears streaming down our cheeks, we happily took her up on her tender invitation.

Once again, joy filled my heart, but not for our ability to get fresh air. Although I was incredibly glad to breathe in the ocean air, my joy came because a tender mercy had been extended to me through the kindness of a stranger. Despite the looming threat of COVID-19, this kind woman and her husband extended a portion of their blessings to those that were not so fortunate. It's her kindness that I will always keep close to my heart.

That gesture represented the beauty of this life. We don't all have the power to control the circumstances we are in, and some are given more than others, whether its talent, money, or just privilege. I'm sure it would be possible for some higher powers to equalize everything by force. But without an individual's ability to voluntarily share, these tender moments would never be possible.

I saw many tender mercies aboard that ship. Whether it was an attendant who went out of their way to provide a little extra, Shelly who brought toilet paper and toothpaste when we ran out, politicians who put forward their best efforts to get us home, or a woman who offered up her balcony so that we could have some fresh air.

Toilet paper Shelly brought us

As I stood on the balcony with this wonderful woman, I looked at the sun setting over the horizon, and a sense of peace came over me. The ocean roared while the salty breeze swept over me, as if to wash away the worries that were weighing me down. A perfect moment in an otherwise disastrous situation. And all of it orchestrated by the hands of others willing to share their kindness toward me. I pulled out my cell phone to capture this exact moment and forever treasure it. It has brought me so much peace through all this. I had Marcie hold her hands up in "heart hands" with the sunset in the distance centered in the heart.

Being powerless often means we are at the mercy of others. Some people take advantage of that, and others use that opportunity to show kindness. I am grateful for those who did not use our desperate situation to their advantage but rather showed true charitable love. I think God gives us those desperate moments to give others an opportunity to extend that same mercy that He does. When they do step up in the face of a devastating situation, it makes the world a beautiful place. That is the lesson that comes from these trying times, a lesson we often forget in the day-to-day activities of our ordinary lives.

Our Protectors

I stood with the woman on the balcony, watching the sun go down. In the distance were the lights of coast-guard vessels, flashing a bright red-and-yellow light. The woman pointed to them. "Looks like we are prisoners on this ship," she said.

At first, I had to agree that it appeared that way. It looked as though they were there to keep any of us from jumping off the ship and swimming to the shore where we could spread the virus. But then another thought came to me. "Maybe they're our protectors," I said.

There were several comments in online forums threatening the ship. San Francisco had not given the okay to dock there, and so we were still sailing in circles, waiting for a place to dock. Some misguided people who had gotten caught up in the fear of the moment had threatened to blow up the ship if it docked in San Francisco. Just as the mercy extended in those desperate times brings beauty, those that indulge in the fears of the moment bring horrible ugliness.

We are constantly beset by these opportunists who take advantage of the weak. When one is powerless, it's reassuring that there are those in the world who are willing to stand against such ugliness. The coast guard may not have been there to keep us on the ship but to keep those that threatened the ship from doing anything to it. They were our protectors.

"I think they are there to keep the crazies away," I said.

Darla looked at me skeptically. "Well, if this quarantine continues any longer, there may be some crazies on the ship."

We laughed. The whole idea of being quarantined on a cruise ship with no harbor to dock was definitely enough to drive anyone crazy. I'm sure that there were many arguing against us, acting in their own best interests. That's the default when we get in these situations. Survival instinct, I guess you would call it. Our base nature is to look out for ourselves. It takes an act of will to go against that desire to choose something more—something of the heart.

When fear takes over, it's hard to make those difficult choices because they require faith in the better nature of others. They also take sacrifice. Whether it's extending food to another when food is already scarce or harboring the disadvantaged when we are disadvantaged ourselves. Choosing faith over fear will never be the path of least resistance. It will always take a conscious and determined choice to be better than we are.

Looking out at the coast-guard ships made me think of all the individuals who worked to help us, especially helping those who were infected. I'm sure they would rather be with their families. I'm also sure they didn't want to risk infecting themselves or their loved ones. Yet they still stepped up to help. You might say they were just doing their job. But in cases like this, I think they were all going above and beyond what their job duties entailed.

Those ships patrolled the harbor all night, sacrificing their sleep so that we could sleep a little more soundly. That is the beauty of humanity. We can be more than our survival instincts. We can choose to look out for one another. That's the whole point of society.

Sure, it benefits us more in the long run and is technically in our best interest to work together. But sometimes in those moments of crisis, people aren't thinking of the long run. It takes more than just good judgment; it takes a good heart.

I choose to see society as a bunch of people flawed and full of mistakes yet still willing to look out for one another. Why? I believe it's because deep down inside, there is good in the majority of us that comes out in the most desperate of times despite the shortcomings of our character. That's what makes life beautiful. Whenever we are willing to stand against fear and despair and choose a better way, we become more than our flawed self. No matter how insignificant our efforts might be, that choice is a big thing in the midst of so many little things.

CHAPTER 4

Basking in the Sun

Sunday, March 8, 2020
Day four in quarantine day seventeen on the ship. Our cruise was sup-
posed to end the day before on Saturday, March 7, 2020.

Before COVID-19 interrupted our vacation, our cruise took us to several Hawaiian Islands. It was an amazing experience, but one of the dearest memories occurred in Hilo. We had met a friend there who helped us get a rental van to tour the island. Hilo is a beautiful city nestled between two volcanoes, Mauna Loa and Mauna Kea, on the largest island, Hawaii. The city is surrounded by lush vegetation, sandy beaches, and some of the most beautiful waterfalls. While there, we hiked to Akaka Falls. My mother's health made it difficult for her to participate in many of the activities, so she stayed by the cars reading a book; while my father and I continued to the falls with the rest of the group. We played in the large heart-shaped leaves that grew there and admired the breathtaking scenery.

Heart leaves

Holding hands

Although the Akaka Falls was one of the most beautiful places I have seen, the memory that stuck most vividly in my mind during that trip occurred on our drive back to the beach. I was riding in the back seat of the van, watching my parents who were seated in front of me. Both of my parents are in their seventies and have been married for most of those years. Although age has humbled their frames and brought its share of difficulties, they still show that love they had the first day they met. While everyone else was admiring the sights, I watched as my parents held hands. I went on the trip to spend time with them, and I would not trade that time for anything. Little moments like that are priceless to me.

We drove to the shoreline down a steep, narrow, winding road with our friends Penny and Susan leading the way in Penny's little Mini Cooper. The sand was black silt, and the water a deep blue. It was truly an awe-inspiring scene. We continued down the road until we came to a dock and boat launch. There were no boats in the water due to high winds and rough waters. Gigantic concrete barriers were positioned out in the water to block the waves from crashing into the boat ramp.

Our friend told us of a tragedy that occurred there seventy-four years ago. A school used to reside on that beach. The school children would often go to the edge of the ocean to collect seashells. While they were there, the sea receded, revealing a treasure trove of shells. It was like nothing they had ever seen. The children, unaware of the danger, rushed out in delight, picking up armfuls of shells, more than they could carry. In the midst of their joyful play, a wave from a nearby tsunami hit the shore. Before they could even run, the water engulfed them and buried the entire school. All that remained were the shattered remnants.

Tsunami pier

The teacher and twenty-five students died that day, along with over a hundred others in the nearby coastal area. I could not imagine the pain suffered by the families of those children. This incident had a huge impact not only on the people of Hilo but across the world. The tragedy spawned an effort to find early detection methods of tsunamis to help save lives. Those efforts led to great progress on how to handle these disasters, and they've saved thousands of lives since. Even the locals learned of the receding tide as a warning sign of the tsunami wave.

Tragedies like the one in Hilo have lasting effects that change the course of society. It may be too early to tell what kind of impact

COVID-19 will have on us as a society, but we can be sure that life will be different because of it. Will we learn from our mistakes or make things worse? Hopefully, we'll learn and become better people because of it.

For me, COVID-19 has brought a greater appreciation for my family and the things that truly matter in life—as I'm sure the tsunami at Hilo did for those who faced the aftermath of that tragedy. We cannot always foresee the dangers that lay in our future. We all get caught off guard when these things happen. It's important to understand that even in the darkest of times, there are lessons to be learned. And in those lessons are the seeds for a brighter tomorrow.

Back at the ship, our embarking was delayed by an emergency medical evacuation. People said that someone on the ship had a heart attack and had to be taken off the ship by paramedics. We were really sad for the passenger and hoped they would be okay and felt bad that this happened to them on such a fun, awesome trip. At the time, we weren't thinking about COVID-19, but after the news of the virus spread on the ship, it brought many questions. Did his heart attack have something to do with the virus? How long did they know that the virus was on the ship? What lay in store for the rest of us?

Looking back, it's easy to see those indicators that might have warned us of a potential hazard. But at that moment, it was impossible to truly fathom what was coming. Maybe there were signs that might have prevented the whole thing, but like those who fell victim to the tsunami, no one knew what to look for. This type of second-guessing is just another trap of despair. Like the need to blame others, this tendency can drive a person into deeper and deeper depression as they look for ways that they could have prevented it.

While in quarantine, I tried not to think about it, but the longer we stayed out at sea, the more I worried. My parents had only packed enough medication for the trip. We were supposed to be at port, heading home, and here we were, stuck in our cabins. Since San Francisco had denied our entry into port, we were floating with no certainty of where we would dock. How long would they last with irregular meals and no medication? Everything was uncertain. I wanted so much to see my parents again, just to prove to myself that they were all right. Let alone my siblings and other family members at home who were riddled with concern.

It's often in those moments when everything seems perfect that the tsunami hits. Those experiences in Hilo were amazing. They provided fond memories with my parents that I cherish. The whole reason for going on this trip was to spend more time with my parents, and now I faced the real possibility that I might actually lose them. That reality hit me hard like a winding blow to my gut. I needed to see them.

Reunion
Monday, March 9, 2020
Day five in quarantine and day eighteen on the ship

On Monday morning, the captain announced that they would resume taking groups up to the top deck. They started earlier this time to ensure that the rest of the decks would all have an opportunity. It was around eight thirty in the morning when they came for us. An attendant knocked at the door and told us we had ten minutes. They instructed us to bring our face masks and wash our hands. I quickly called my parents cabin to see if they were going out too. My dad answered with an overly excited yes. My dad, being the patriarch of this little flock, also instructed us to bring a jacket as the top deck often got windy.

With hearts pounding and hands shaking, we frantically scrambled around the room to get ready. When a typical morning took at least an hour of preparation, ten minutes hardly seemed enough. I brushed through my hair quickly as I gathered my stuff together. Grabbing my mask, I ran out the door along with Marcie. In the hallway, there was a line of people. Every person was two meters apart. This was a new thing the ship had implemented at the request of the CDC. It was a fairly unfamiliar term at the time called *social distancing*.

I imagine that term is well ingrained in the minds of all of us by now, but at the time, the idea was strange. We did what the attendants asked and went in line two meters from the next person. People in full personal protective equipment (PPE) greeted us as we made our way to the stairwell. They asked us several questions about any symptoms we may have had such as fever, coughing, chest congestions, etc.— basically, anything that might indicate exposure to COVID-19.

My heart was pounding so hard I thought it was going to jump right out of my chest. The whole experience was surreal, different from anything I had ever experienced. It was like I was living out one of those horror movies about an outbreak. While it did not serve to calm my concerns about the situation, at the time, I was more focused on getting to the top deck and seeing my parents again. The top deck was called the Lido deck. We had previously arranged to meet each other on the starboard side by the outdoor pool.

After they surveyed us, they allowed us passage to the stairwell, which would take us to the top deck. We climbed several flights before reaching the top deck, the whole time keeping our distance from one another. Since we had spent nearly four days in the cabin, we were not used to that kind of exertion. The climb was an effort even though we had so much energy running through us from excitement to see the others. As we reached the upper decks, I saw the sun and the ocean. In the far-off distance, I saw the Golden Gate Bridge, signifying our proximity to San Francisco. I was told it was around twenty to thirty nautical miles away.

Ship circling outside of San Francisco Bay

Me and Marcie going outside

It wasn't until that moment that I realized just how close we were. The ship was outside of the bay, and still, we could not leave the ship. We floated aimlessly with no destination. There's something disheartening about being so close to shore and yet not being able to dock. It was like we had been cast off, orphaned from the rest of the nation. No one wanted to take responsibility for us. No one wanted to chance spreading the virus in their city. In the minds of the nation, this new virus was on par with the Black Plague, and no one wanted to take a chance. For all anyone knew, we were all infected. After all, we were floating around for two weeks in a giant petri dish.

After what seemed an eternity, I finally reached the Lido deck. I was breathing heavy, but happy. I walked out on the deck, closed my eyes, and spread my face to the sun. Its warmth embraced me like a soft cocoon. I drew in a deep breath of fresh ocean air. My lungs pulled it in gratefully. It was the most wonderful moment.

Opening my eyes once more, I squinted against the foreign light to scan the crowd for my parents. I noticed Marcie running out ahead of me. In the distance was Quin, her brother, and his wife Susan. They weren't my parents, but they were part of our group and might as well have been family. After all, we had known one another for over three decades. Tears welled in my eyes as my heart nearly burst with gratitude.

Quin, Susan and Marcie hugging

Marcie leapt into Quin and Susan's arms as they greeted her. They hugged one another for a long time. We were all crying at that point. I ran over and joined in the embrace. I cannot express the joy I felt at that moment. It was as if the whole thing was a nightmare we were waking up from and everything was normal again. Then reality struck with its heavy boot.

"Hey, stop that!" an attendant yelled. "You need to keep at least two meters apart." Her voice was gruff as she scolded us. "You're not part of this family," she demanded. I'm not sure how she knew that I wasn't technically part of their family. But somehow, she did.

I backed up against the edge of the raised pool. My heart felt so heavy in that moment that I couldn't bear it any longer. My legs gave out as I slid down the wall and collapsed onto the deck. Sitting with my back against the wall, I buried my head in my knees and burst into tears. I couldn't help it. I just sat there alone and sobbed uncontrollably.

It wasn't just the fact that I had been scolded as if I were a child. It was a combination of mounting emotions and fatigue. I had tried to keep it together. But there I was expecting a reunion with my parents, but they were nowhere to be found. And now I couldn't even hug my friends. I felt so alone. The tsunami had come, and it was threatening to drown me in its wake.

"They are really worried about you," a voice said. It was Susan. I looked up at her, embarrassed, and could barely make out her face through my blurry tears. She knelt beside me. "By *they*, I mean the lady that yelled at you." She pointed at the attendant, who was watching us at a distance. Susan put an arm around me, and we cried together.

There are things that the human soul needs more than sunlight and fresh air. I would say that we need it more than food or water. We all need a kind voice and the feel of human contact. No one can last long alone. All the devices in the world cannot take the place of that human-to-human connection. We cannot enforce distancing between people without some consequence.

As I sat with Susan on that deck, the need for connection became clearer to me than it ever had. Just having her presence there made all the difference. I don't know why. We barely spoke; we just sat and cried together. And it was exactly what I needed at that moment. People need people.

You can decide to be positive and not give in to fears, but even the best of us can't keep it up forever. Eventually, the world gets to us, and where do we turn? My go-to is often God, but I think even He realized that prayer was not enough. It's not good for us to be alone. We need friends and family. Being able to sit with Susan and just cry got a lot of pent-up emotion out that I wasn't able to process before.

"Hey, look who's here," Susan exclaimed.

In the distance, I saw my parents slowly making their way across the deck. I squealed with delight as I leapt from the deck floor and raced over to them. I paused a few meters away from them and looked over to the attendant to see if she would yell at me again.

Hugging my dad

Hugging my mom

She smiled softly and nodded in approval. I think she felt bad about her gruffness before. I leapt forward and embraced both of them with such joy as I've ever felt. From behind us, Marcie and Quin broke out into one of Otis Redding's songs, "(Sittin' On) The Dock of the Bay."

> *Sittin' in the mornin' sun*
> *I'll be sittin' when the evenin' comes*
> *Watchin' the ships roll in*
> *Then I watch 'em roll away again*
> *I'm sittin' on the dock of the bay*
> *Watchin' the tide, roll away*
> *I'm sittin' on the dock of the bay*
> *Wastin' time*

We all joined in and started dancing. We were together, and we were happy once more. I looked over and caught the same attendant who scolded me previously, making a call on her radio. Our antics drew some more unwanted attention. An official in a white maritime uniform scattered us, telling us that we had to be apart. Once again, we were scolded—this time, by someone more official. Social distance strikes again. At that point, we didn't care. We were just glad to be together. So we started walking laps with the rest of the people around the deck.

My mom couldn't walk too much, so she sat down by one of the windows and enjoyed the view; while my dad and I walked around the deck together.

"So how are you and Mom doing?" I asked, nudging my dad with my shoulder.

He smiled. "All right, I suppose."

I stared at him with discerning eyes. He looked back at me as if holding something back. My dad was not one to talk about problems. I'm not much either, hence my breakdown on the deck. We tend to hold things inside and not talk about them. I continued to stare as if conducting an interrogation. Eventually, he broke.

"I'm a little concerned for your mother's health," he replied.

"Have you gotten your medication?" I asked.

"We filled out the forms but still haven't heard anything."

"Well, they have to get you your medications," I demanded. "You can't go without them."

"I'm sure they will be there when we dock," he assured me.

"Whenever that is," I murmured.

My parents both took medications—my dad for his heart condition and my mom for her diabetes and high blood pressure. As if having a pandemic on the ship wasn't enough, there was the threat that they weren't going to get their medication.

My dad put his hand on my shoulder and squeezed lovingly. "Don't worry," he said. "It'll all work out." One of our sayings on this trip was "Everything works out for Marcie." We felt this was true for all of us as well.

That was my dad. He was a rock to me. It didn't matter how bad the storms got. He would stand fixed and calm, saying, "It'll all work out." His assurance that things would work out was not based on a naive notion but was a deep-rooted faith, etched by a lifetime of experience. He had gone through many difficulties in his life, but he had seen his way through with his faith in God. He was always spiritual and was baptized into the Church of Jesus Christ of Latter-day Saints at age fifty-five by Mark. At the age of seventy-three, he had had plenty of time to test the idea. Still, he was just as sure as the first time I heard those words from him as a child.

The attendants began to herd people back down below deck. The maritime man gruffly and impatiently told us to catch up to the people in front of us. I quickly turned to him and sternly informed him we were not with those people and wanted to maintain our two meters. He was not amused. My dad walked over to my mom and tenderly offered her his hand. She stood and placed hers in his, and together they descended the steps to the lower cabin. I was reminded of that moment in Hilo, watching them hold hands. I was grateful that they had each other.

We were only on the deck for twenty or thirty minutes, but it was a great feeling. Maybe it was the fresh air. Maybe it was the sunshine. But I think there is something with being around others that energizes us. Feeling the tangible love of family is food for the soul that cannot be replaced. I don't know that I would have been able to make it through the rest of our stay in quarantine without that experience of being able to go on the deck and see my family. It gave me the strength to keep going.

Safe Harbor

Returning to our rooms after the wonderful reunion on the upper deck was perhaps the hardest thing I had to do. Still, the experience gave me a renewed energy to persevere. It quelled many of my concerns, especially about the condition of my parents. But at the same time, new concerns arose. What if my mom and dad didn't get their medications? How would they manage?

In my haste to leave the room, I realized I forgot my key card to get back in. Luckily, Marcie had hers. But that didn't help much since for some reason, our door would not unlock. The steward was getting irritated with us for continuing to stand in the hallway. We told him it wasn't working. He frustratingly grabbed his own master key, commenting that we were doing it wrong and had to swipe in the right place. This made us feel dumb. He proceeded to swipe it across the screen. He tried several times to no avail when another steward came over to try his master key card. Nothing worked.

One steward said he would go get his supervisor while the other kept trying. The supervisor came to try and also couldn't get it to work. She was really nice to us though, and I made sure to let the cruise line know. This took about fifteen minutes, but we didn't care. It kept us out of our cramped room for a while. Finally, they decided to go to find an actual metal key, which was probably in some old drawer covered in dust and spiderwebs. This is how I pictured it, at least. They unlocked the doors to our prison cell once again and had to replace the batteries in the electronic key system.

I had my nightly FaceTime with my husband. Things like FaceTime became a lifeline for me. I was so grateful that the captain made sure that we had the internet; it was my only connection to home. The captain was making sure there was enough bandwidth for everyone. He arranged to have it increased several times throughout our quarantine. My husband spent most of his days at work but spent all his downtime helping us get home. While I was in quarantine, he was on the phone talking to me or helping me with my side project of contacting as many influential people as we could find to help me and my group get back home. He often seemed more determined than I did.

Marcie was in the bathroom sending voice messages and Marco Polos back and forth to family and laughing. We affectionately called the bathroom the phone booth. It was the one place in the room where we could go to have a private conversation.

I tried to do little things to stay connected to home. Back at home, we had a thermostat connected to the internet. In our house, the thermostat was a contested ground between my husband and I and our children. We would constantly battle over it. We liked keeping things cooler in the winter and more energy efficient; the kids liked things warmer. So when I heard that there was a late spring snowstorm back home, I used the app to turn the heat up for them. It was like my little way of letting them know that I was still there for them.

But none of the phone calls, face chats, or apps took the place of being there. I couldn't wait to get home. So when the news came that night that we would be docking, I was excited.

The captain, in his British voice, sounded overhead. "As part of our coordination with federal state and local authorities, an agreement has been reached to bring our ship into the port of Oakland tomorrow."

I let out a squeal of elation. Finally, there was a light at the end of the tunnel. There's something about having that light ahead of you that helps you continue on. We all believed it would happen eventually, but there was no indication of when. Now we had a definite day and location. I was more excited in that moment about going home than I was when I decided to go on the trip.

"Just to say that again, agreement has been reached to bring our ship into the port of Oakland tomorrow. While the exact time of our arrival has not been completely finalized, we anticipate arriving sometime tomorrow afternoon. After docking, we will then begin a disembarkation process specified by authorities that is likely to take several days."

"Several days?" I exclaimed. What could they possibly need to do that would take several days? I had imagined that they would just let us off the ship and we would fly back home.

The announcement continued, "Again, the disembarkation process is still being finalized by US and state of California health authorities…"

The rest of the announcement went over points of the plan that concerned different passengers and their status going forward. Those from California would stay in a federally operated California isolation facility. Those from other states would go to other facilities on military bases across the US. There was no indication of what would be done at those facilities or how long we would be staying there. Despite the disturbing thought of staying in an isolation facility on some military base, it was at least a step forward and closer to home.

As I went to bed that night, I thought over my day. A practice that my friend Liz who drove us all over Kauai on our first island port shared with us. She called it her *rose, thorn,* and *bud.* Each day, she would think of one *rose,* something good that happened that day. Then she would think of one *thorn,* something that wasn't so good and what you learned from it. Finally, she would end on the *bud,* something hopeful to look forward to for the rest of your journey.

Me and my friend Liz

After Liz told me about her "rose, thorn, and bud" approach, I decided to start doing the same. Throughout the trip, I had many roses and buds. Spending time with family, being invited to participate in the fashion show on the ship, dancing with my dad, and meeting new friends—these are all beautiful memories that made the trip special.

Now that I was in quarantine, I needed those roses more than ever. My rose every night was FaceTime with my husband, but that night, I had many other roses to add. I got time outside in the fresh air and sun. I had precious time with parents and confirmation that they are doing well in spite of everything. And now I had a beautiful bud to look forward to tomorrow. We would be docking in Oakland. It was a good day.

I ignored the thorns. Maybe that was a mistake. But at the time, I had enough thorns to worry about. I didn't need to dwell on them. So I just thought of the roses I had been given that day—and the new blossoms the buds would provide tomorrow.

Waimanalo beach, Oahu

CHAPTER 5

The Waiting Game

Monday, March 9–Thursday, March 12, 2020
Days five through eight of quarantine and days eighteen through twenty-one on the ship.

Waiting is rarely easy, but it's still a necessary part of life. We were hoping to get back on land. But the docking was delayed until the following morning, and the disembarkation process took several days just as they said. We didn't get another chance to go up to the top deck, but the woman across the way left her door open so we could get some fresh air and sunlight. Our days passed as they had previously in quarantine. We continued to watch the news, chat with our family and friends, and wait.

The ship's crew tried to help in passing the time. They offered an entertainment channel from crew members of the ship like the cruise directors, staff, and entertainers. They would have a variety of games like trivia. They sent around little packets in envelopes with pieces of paper cut into little squares that were colored. One of the staff members demonstrated on the entertainment channel how to make fun things with origami-like hearts. There was also yoga that we attempted to follow along with in our cramped quarters.

Princess craft packet

Marcie snuck over to her brother's room, which was about ten doors down. I understood why. We got along great, but I couldn't replace the comfort of a sibling. I think those trips to her brother's room helped her get through a very difficult situation. However, it left me alone for extended periods of time. Being alone in the room was difficult; but I tried to find ways to cope like yoga and, on one occasion, a personal dance party. It provided exercise and made me happy—two things I desperately needed. I also spent a lot of time on my artwork. I have enjoyed art my entire life. It was calming and therapeutic. I drew a lot of pictures of loved ones and Christ since they were the most comforting to others.

I often talked to my husband, Mark, on FaceTime. I tried not to unload on him though. My being away from him was hard enough. I didn't want to add to the stress. For the most part, I could put on a happy face and be positive, and that would help me feel more positive inside. However, there were days that were harder than others. One particularly hard day, I broke out into song. It's all I could do not to cry. While I was talking to Mark, Rachel Platten's "Fight Song" came on the music channel, and I just sang along with it. I kind of adopted that song as my personal mantra several years ago, and it still holds true today.

Like a small boat
On the ocean
Sending big waves
Into motion
Like how a single word
Can make a heart open
I might only have one match
But I can make an explosion

And all those things I didn't say
Wrecking balls inside my brain
I will scream them loud tonight
Can you hear my voice this time?

This is my fight song
Take back my life song
Prove I'm alright song
My power's turned on
Starting right now I'll be strong
I'll play my fight song
And I don't really care if nobody else believes
'Cause I've still got a lot of fight left in me

I needed those reminders that I could be strong, especially as conditions deteriorated. Food was getting scarcer, and our choices, which were originally quite large, dwindled down to no choice at all. They stopped sending menus altogether. You got what you got, and that was it. The food we did receive was less than appetizing. Runny eggs at breakfast, wilted lettuce in the salad, no seasoning or condiments—just bland food. They sent cold coffee, not that it mattered. I'm not a coffee drinker, so I just dumped it out.

I knew that things were difficult, and supplies were short. We were on the ship much longer than was anticipated, so I can't entirely blame the cruise line. Plans were constantly up in the air as we waited to hear word of disembarking. As the captain referred to it, everything was fluid. Still, the combination of being kept in a small dark room with no fresh air or sunshine, having barely any edible food, and not being able to see my parents who were just down the hall culminated into an emotional breakdown. As time stretched on with no word of when my turn would be to leave the ship, I decided to reach out. The ship had a mental-health hotline for those who were struggling.

On one particularly hard day, I was alone in the room. I had just received word that my mother's medication still hadn't arrived, and I was concerned about her health. I felt scared, vulnerable, and weak. I needed someone to talk to, someone to reassure me everything was going to be okay. In desperation, I dialed the number.

I just wanted to vent my concerns to someone. I thought they might have a new perspective that might help our situation. Or at least they would have something uplifting for me. But it wasn't what I expected. They took my name and information, and I started talking. It was nice to talk to someone about it, but I didn't know this person. I had no connection with them. And I'm not generally the type of person to discuss my problems with a stranger. I soon realized this wasn't working, and I regretted calling; but I didn't know how to tell the person on the other end that I just wasn't getting what I needed.

Just then, a call came from a reporter, and I used it as an excuse to hang up. I expected that the person on the other end of the hotline would try to keep me on the line or attempt to contact me later, but I didn't hear back from them. I'm not sure what they did with my information or if they were even interested in keeping tabs on those who were struggling emotionally. It seemed like that would have been something they should be aware of; but perhaps there were too many people going through similar issues, and they just didn't know how to handle that many people. Maybe there were just too many to keep track of. In any case, I'm glad they didn't call me back. I don't know what more I would've said to them.

After the phone call, I decided to turn to a different source—God. I prayed with all my heart for some help or at least comfort. Alone in that small room amid one of the most distressing events in my life, peace came. I can't explain how talking to God was different from talking to that person on the phone. It wasn't like God came to have a personal counseling session with me. But the feeling I received was real. It was like the feeling I got when my dad would put his arm around me as a child to comfort me when I was struggling. It was quiet, warm, and reassuring. That heavenly assurance from a divine father was enough to keep me going.

God's interventions on my behalf were often simple and subtle, but they did not go unrecognized. It wasn't just times of despair where He comforted me. I know He had given me the small impressions I received previous to the trip that helped me, like taking my own medications, soap, and shampoo. When these things started to run out, I was happy to have them with me. Little things like that went a long way to helping me through.

I'm also sure His divine hand was there in getting me home. Although aid often came through the actions of others on my behalf, it was apparent it was by His design. It just couldn't have worked out as perfectly as it did without His help. I may never know all the ways that God helped me get home, but it was enough for me to know there was someone looking out for me. That faith has always gotten me through the most desperate of times, and it got me through that time on the *Grand Princess*.

Mark Gets Desperate

Despite my best effort to put on a happy face with my husband, he knew that I was struggling. Mark did all he could to cheer me up. When things were particularly hard for me, he got permission from our local church leader to perform a blessing over a video call.

In the church that I belong to, every worthy male has the ability to perform priesthood blessings. This is done by laying the hands on the person who is afflicted or in need of comfort and is done in the name of Jesus Christ. It is unusual to perform a blessing over the phone, but in desperate times, it is allowed.

I set the phone next to my head, and he proceeded to give me a blessing. I desperately needed comfort and was grateful to have a husband who could perform such a blessing. He placed his hands on my head and gave me words of encouragement and relief. The words were just what I needed, but more important was the feeling that I received. As soon as the blessing started, a feeling of peace came over me. I could actually feel his hands on my head. When he ended the blessing I opened my eyes and looked up to see the lampshade gently resting upon my head. I felt it was God's way of telling me that all was well. Everything was going to be fine.

Mark made it his job every day to stir the pot, as he would call it, trying to make something happen. It started with phone calls to government officials and the cruise line. He called anyone who would listen, trying to get their help to get us home. He found people who knew people who, in turn, had connections to other people. It was an endless chain of bureaucratic runaround. There was finger-pointing from one office to another, from one state authority to another, and then to federal authorities. Everyone said they would do what they could, but none seemed to have the final decision on the situation. Finding someone to solve the problem seemed hopeless as it often does with government institutions.

As the days continued and there was still no word of when I would be getting off the ship, he became more desperate. Feeling that all his calls were in vain, he decided to take things to a new level of crazy. Mark came up with his Plan A. He was going to get on a plane and fly to Oakland. From there, he would rent a Suburban and drive to the dock. There, he would make as much commotion and noise that he could muster, anything short of violence. He figured he would at least get on the news and bring this ordeal to the forefront of everybody's mind. He would demand my release and force the government to act.

Mark visited his parents in the assisted living center where they lived and told them of the plan. After getting his father's blessing, he went home and looked for flights to Oakland. Luckily, he had the sense to call me before booking the flight. While he was going over Plan A with me, I thought, *Is it really going to come down to this?* I envisioned my husband on the six o'clock news being tackled by port authorities while screaming, "Let my wife go!"

Just as I was telling him how absurd the plan was in an attempt to stop him from going forward with it, I heard a knock at the door. It was a ship attendant handing me a group of six cream-colored luggage tags for us to place on our checked bags in preparation for us to disembark. I thought I was finally going to leave the ship. Mark and I cried with joy over the news and laughed at his almost disastrous plan to rescue me. It may not have been the best plan, but it showed how much he cared about me and wanted me home. I would say he is my knight in shining armor, but a Hawaiian shirt is more his style. I was just glad for the fortuitous timing of that knock at the door; I didn't know if I could have convinced him not to go through with his plan otherwise.

I called the information desk to find out more about the tags since there were six of them and we each only had one bag to put the tags on. I figured somehow they had sent all of our tags to my room, so I was trying to find a way to redistribute the tags to the rest of our group as we had previously written instructions on our paperwork that we were all to go together when leaving the ship. To my dismay, they informed me the tags were only for Marcie, and I would receive my own tags when it was my turn to leave. I then realized I would not be leaving and would be all alone. I was crushed and wondered why we weren't going together. I called Marcie, who was in her brother's room at the time, and gave her the good news; she was going home.

Saying Goodbye
Day seven in quarantine and day twenty on the ship

Another day was nearing its end when finally, the rest of us were given our tags to place on our luggage. Marcie's tags were the cream-colored tags, and the rest of our group received yellow tags. We packed our belongings and placed our bags outside the door as instructed then waited. We were supposed to receive a phone call telling us when to go. Marcie's call came first. I still had hope that we would be going together, but that didn't happen. Marcie was leaving on her own.

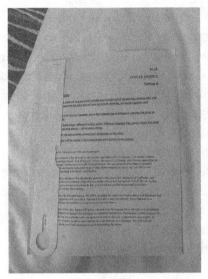

Yellow Tags

Happiness seeds

Before leaving, she gave me and everyone in our group *happy seeds*. They were round painted porcelain clumps with a smiley face on them. They were an idea from Mark Borella, a sculptor. He would always have little clumps of clay leftover. Rather than throwing them away, he started making them into smiles. He would share them with his friends by the handful, asking them to pass them along to others and calling them *Seeds of Happiness*. The colorful seeds have a large smile on them to make people smile. It was a way to sow happiness in the world.

Marcie had planned on giving them to us on the day we left the ship, but things didn't work out that way. She asked us to keep them someplace where we could see them and remember all the good laughs we shared. The seeds were a sign of our solidarity in an extremely challenging time, reminding us that despite the hardships endured, there were still many wonderful memories from the trip.

Marcie texted us about her experience disembarking. She had thought that she was going straight to her home in Las Vegas, but she was rerouted to the Miramar Marine Corps Base in San Diego. I had been told by my state officials that I would be going straight home to Utah. In fact, I was told not to go with anyone else, including the CDC. When Marcie got her call and I didn't, I thought that perhaps the delay was due to officials in Utah making arrangements for my parents and I to go there. Although Marcie being sent to Miramar should have made me doubt the possibility of going straight home, I was still convinced it would happen. Perhaps it's one of those things that you tell yourself to keep hope alive. I could stand to stay one more night on the ship as long as I could be home the next night. I had no reason to believe otherwise, so I continued to believe that tomorrow I would be home.

In the meantime, it was time to express my gratitude to those that had helped me on the ship. At the beginning of our cruise, Marcie came up with this way to thank those that had made our trip special. She brought these cards in the shape of hearts. They were small, about four inches by four inches. Nothing too extravagant, just something to let the staff and those we were traveling with know that we appreciated them.

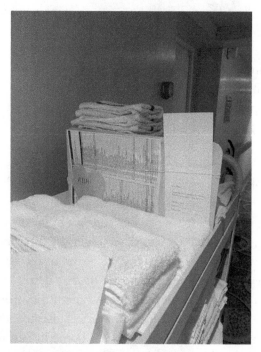

Heart card

For example, on our first formal dining night, the food and atmosphere were so amazing. Out of appreciation for the evening, we gave the person in charge a heart card. He thanked us profusely. I don't think the staff generally were recognized for the effort that they put into making the activities aboard the ship special. But like anyone else, they genuinely enjoyed the recognition and remembered those that had shown their appreciation. From the time that we gave Genel that card until the end of the trip, anytime we dined in his hall, he would bring us extra treats like special appetizers that he made just for us. He enjoyed our feedback and was willing to provide us with something special all because we expressed our appreciation.

I believe the majority of people are that way. We all serve in some capacity, whether in the work that we do or in our relationships with loved ones. Most work go unnoticed. But those who serve still continue to serve—whether they're a banquet attendant, line worker, or even a parent. They do it because that's their job and what they signed up to do. When they do get recognized, it validates that their work means something, and they're willing to put more of themselves into it. Too often in life, people hold back in their work because they either feel it doesn't matter or that people won't appreciate what they do. By the simple gesture of giving that card, we showed Genel that his efforts did matter. From then on, he was willing to open up and show us more of his creations—more of himself. He was from Romania, and he would spend six months on the ship then go home to his family for three months. He was a great man and friend to us. We will forever treasure knowing him.

We had similar experiences with waiters and others who served us. One set of waiters were named Mario and Luigi. I don't know if those were made up or if those were their actual names. In any case, we had a good laugh about it with them. They were so nice to us, so we gave them a card with a little note to each of them. You could tell it meant a lot to them. Every time we gave a card, it not only brightened the person's day but they were also more open and comfortable telling us about themselves and letting us into their lives. There were thirty-two cards total, which we split between everyone in our group. We gave away all but a handful of them, which I planned on handing out before I left.

Captain thank you heart card

On my last day, I wrote a letter to the captain. It was a simple thank you for his work in trying to keep us safe during our time in lockdown. I know the situation wasn't ideal for him either, and I wanted him to know that I recognized his efforts to get us through this difficult time. I put down my room number and name, along with the room numbers and names of the rest of our group. I wanted him to know that it wasn't just me, that we were all grateful. The next morning, I placed the card outside my door with instructions to the attendant to deliver it to the captain.

A few hours later, the captain came over the intercom with his announcements. Toward the end of his speaking, he paused. With his voice slightly choked, he expressed his gratitude for all those who had been supportive of him and the crew during this trying time. I knew then that he had received my card along with many others.

Sharing gratitude with someone opens them up to expressing their gratitude as well. Nothing smooths a tense situation like a sincere expression of appreciation. We all play our parts in these unexpected and trying events, and some of them are more difficult than others. It has become too easy and too frequent for the critics of our actions to be heard the loudest. And not frequent enough that those who share genuine appreciation are heard. If we want to heal as a society, we need to start by being willing to share our gratitude for one another and especially for God.

More Waiting
Day eight in quarantine and day twenty-one on the ship

The next day came with no call, and I continued to wait alone in my room. I still held on to the idea that I was going home to Utah. For three days, this continued. By the third day, I was done. *I can't spend another day on this ship*, I screamed to myself. *I just can't do it.* My parents felt the same way.

Lunch came and went with no word. Then I got a text from Quin and Susan that they had received their call. They were leaving. We had the same tags but still received no call. They texted us that they had been standing out on the dock for several hours with nowhere to sit but were now finally getting on the shuttle bus. This was about two in the afternoon. This made me nervous. Why wouldn't they call us too? Had they forgotten about us? I contacted the guest services, trying to figure out why we would not be going together. I thought perhaps there had been a mistake. The attendant assured us that they would call us when they were ready for us. I hung up and continued to wait.

Susan and Quin texted us that the bus had left, and they were headed to Miramar as well. That's when it hit me that I would not be going home. At that point, I didn't care where I went as long as it was off the ship. My parents hadn't been called yet, so I figured maybe there was still a chance that we would be going to Utah together. I tried to convince myself that was the reason for it taking so long.

The afternoon came, and still nothing. Then around seven o'clock in the evening, the phone to our room rang. It was the call to go down to mid-ship level 5. A feeling of relief rushed over me like a drenching downpour. My nerves were frayed, and my body was tired and weak. I grabbed the last of my things and gave the room one last walk-through to make sure nothing was left behind then went to my parent's cabin.

At this point, we had no idea where we were going. I clung to the last shred of hope that we would be going to Utah and that I would be home in a couple of hours. I helped my parents out the door and to the elevator. It was so good to finally be together again. As worn out as I was, I couldn't imagine the impact this was having on them. They still hadn't received all their medications, and it had been days since their supply ran low or altogether out. My mom had been rationing her insulin to dangerously low levels. My dad finally received his heart medication but would likely run out again. If we could at least get home, they would have extra medication there.

We walked down the ramp of the ship with the others who had been called to disembark. The social distancing rules were no longer being enforced. I think at this point, people didn't care whether they got COVID-19 or not. They just wanted to get off the ship. At the bottom of the ramp was a large white tent with workers dressed in white gowns, their faces covered with big plastic face shields. They were wearing gloves on their hands and booties over their shoes with tape around their wrists and ankles to completely isolate themselves from any possible germs that could be floating around.

They interviewed us one by one to see if we had any symptoms. They checked our IDs and took our temperatures. Luckily, our temperatures were normal. At the time, I had no idea what they did with those with high fevers or symptoms of the virus. I was later told those that were sick were sent to a base in California. As soon as they were done with their screening process, they escorted us to the bus.

The Health and Human Services (HHS) back home had told me that the people at the docks might try to get me to go to one of the military quarantine sites. They told me that the governor of Utah had already made arrangements for my parents and me to be picked up by plane and taken to Utah. They instructed me that if they insisted on us going anywhere else to put my foot down and tell them that we are supposed to be going straight home to Utah.

I turned to the worker and asked, "Where are we going?"

The worker was in the process of herding people onto the bus and gave me little attention.

"Excuse me," I said, trying to get his attention. "I was told that I'm supposed to go to Utah."

He looked at me and smiled. "You're going to Dobbins."

Where's Dobbins? I thought. I had never heard of the place, but I knew it wasn't in Utah. The state officials I had talked to told me not to go anywhere but to Utah.

"No," I exclaimed. "I'm not supposed to go to Dobbins. Health and Human Services told me I would be going straight to Utah with my parents. The governor has arranged for a plane to take us home."

The worker laughed. "No, you're not," he said. "I'm from the HHS, and I'm telling you you're going to Dobbins."

"We're not supposed to be going there," I insisted. "The HHS told me to put my foot down and tell you that we're going straight home."

The worker was losing his patience at this point. "I'm sorry, but I am the HHS. And I'm telling you to get on the bus. You're going to Dobbins." His face was stern. He was not going to budge on the matter. I was going to Dobbins, or else I was going who knows where.

Seeing his frustrations, I chose not to push the matter. I didn't want to get arrested. Things were tense, and I wasn't sure what they would do to me; so I got on the bus. I didn't want to go, but I hoped that things would get worked out on the way to the airport. I was wrong.

At the airport, there was a charter plane waiting for us, but still we waited on the bus for several hours. When we were finally let off the bus, a National Guardsman directed us to a line of porta-potties. "Everybody needs to go to the bathroom before boarding the plane," the man said. "It's going to be a long flight, and we weren't supposed to use the bathroom on the plane."

There was no discussing other options. They told us where to go and what to do, and we were expected to just follow instructions. No one objected. No one fell out of line. I think we were all too broken-down and tired from the experience to even raise a voice. It was late, and we had an entire flight to a place we didn't even know.

"Where are we going?" I asked the worker as I stepped onto the plane.

"Georgia," he replied. "Dobbins Air Reserve Base in Marietta, Georgia."

Georgia! I was about to go across the entire country. I was supposed to be going home. This was not what was supposed to happen. I had tried so hard to stay positive, but the reality of the situation threatened to extinguish any hope that was left in me. I was crushed. Home seemed even farther than it was before.

On the plane, my body continued to feel uneasy. The whole experience was surreal. I had never in my life thought that I would be in a situation like that. We were herded like sheep to an end we knew nothing of. It was degrading and terrifying. I don't know if it was the lack of substantial food, the fatigue, or the stress; but my body finally gave out on the plane. I collapsed into my seat. My mind spinning, thinking of what was about to happen to us. Why were they doing this? Why couldn't we just go home? We weren't sick. We didn't have any symptoms. We might just get sick being around people who were sick.

As the engines started and the plane began to move, the realization came that my time in quarantine had just begun. I was going to spend two weeks in Georgia.

CHAPTER 6

The Final Trial

Friday, March 13, 2020
Day nine in quarantine.

It was nearly a five-hour trip to Georgia. My dad sat next to me, and my mom had the window seat. Her blood sugar was all out of whack from not eating and having no access to insulin. She had a terrible headache on takeoff, and it persisted throughout the flight. Luckily, I brought my own Tylenol and Ibuprofen to give to her. It was enough to take the edge off and help her get some long needed sleep.

I struggled to find a comfortable position to sleep and really had little to no success. I've never been able to sleep on an airplane sitting up, and the seats on the charter plane were not like those on commercial planes. They didn't recline at all, had no bending head-rests, and were really just basically uncomfortable. I had a neck roll that I used to prop up my head. However, this would only work for a few minutes, and then I would have to readjust my positioning. As we were nearing the last hour of the flight and starting our descent, I felt a pop in my head. Pain was searing through my skull, and my stomach was getting nauseated.

I have a history of chronic migraines that would come and go ever since a car accident I had in January of 2010. The migraine was the result of a neck injury that I received during the accident, caus-ing three disks in my neck to protrude into my spine. For two years after that accident, I suffered from daily migraines. Over time, with the help of healthy living, stretching, and water aerobics at Surf-n-Swim, they all but disappeared. Soon they were just an occasional annoyance that was manageable with typical medication. But this migraine was much more severe than any of the others I had ever experienced. Maybe it was from anxiety, maybe it was the inability to sleep correctly or the sudden change in cabin pressure, or maybe it was a combination of them all—the perfect trifecta.

I pulled the bottle of Dramamine from my purse. Twisting off the cap, I took out one pill and with a quick tilt of my head, swallowed it down. I hoped that would be enough to alleviate the nausea. Suddenly, a searing pain shot through my head, and I felt like I was going to pass out. It was as if something had just burst in my head. I had never felt anything like it. After the pop, I felt what I can only describe as sharp glass running through the blood vessels in my head. The sensation surged from the top of my head downward behind my eyes and nasal passage.

I was completely subdued by the pain and was unable to focus on anything else. In my delirious and exhausted state, I thought that maybe they had done something to me. I didn't know what or even how, just that someone had done this to me. I know this paranoia was just part of the migraine, but at the time, it caused me to panic. I thought that someone had actually done something to my brain.

I motioned to a woman dressed in full quarantine gear who was checking on the passengers. She came to my side. "Is everything all right?" she asked.

"I think I'm going to pass out," I said. My speech was strained. I couldn't think coherently. It was a struggle just to make words to explain what was happening.

Worried, the woman looked toward the back of the plane. "I'll be right back," she said. She walked to the rear of the plane to talk to another disaster volunteer. The two of them returned and helped me out of my seat, walking me carefully back to the rear of the plane where three empty seats awaited. They laid me down with my pillow.

I laid there, my head tingling with sharp jagged stabs. My vision soon blurred, and everything fell into a thick black as if I were falling down a dark well. My body felt cold, and I began to shake. Tears were streaming down my face. Although I couldn't see the other passengers, I felt their concern and worry for me and for themselves. I'm sure they were wondering what was going on and if it was a symptom of COVID-19.

The plane touched down in Georgia around five thirty in the morning. The two disaster volunteers who helped me previously had found a wheelchair for me to sit in while they carried me off the plane. My vision was still blurry, and my head still hurt. I wasn't able to focus on anything around me. I saw about four individuals helping me down the long flight of stairs down to the tarmac. In my delirious state, I kept apologizing. I felt so bad for the inconvenience I was making. I tried to get up a few times to manage on my own but quickly fell back down in the chair. I was too weak and disoriented to even stand. Every time I tried, the sensation of passing out returned, so I remained in the chair and let them do their job.

Just landed in Marietta Georgia

I wasn't sure where they were taking me. I remember it was still dark outside and slightly raining and someone directed those that were helping me to take me to a place away from the rest of the crowd. I think they wanted to check me out, to make sure I didn't have a stroke or something. They took me to a tent in a corner of a spacious building just off the runway. It may have been a hanger, though I wasn't sure. The lights overhead were blindingly bright. They made the pain in my head even more intense.

The two people helping me were arguing over what to do with me. They were concerned that I was infected with COVID-19 and would be a danger to the others. Plus, there were different protocols to use if I was infected. I assured them that it was just a migraine. I turned my head to show them how my neck had made a popping sound; just then, my neck made another popping sound. I don't know if it was a pinched nerve or something else, but as soon as my neck popped a second time, my migraine started to get less intense. I was suddenly able to see where I was and who was treating me.

I still don't know what caused the migraine and what caused the popping in my neck. I imagine it had something to do with my previous neck injury, but I don't know why it acted up at that moment. I'm just grateful that it eased up a bit before they decided to take me to a hospital. Perhaps another one of heaven's favors on my behalf.

Once my senses came back and the pain subsided, they asked me about myself. My name? What kind of medical needs I had? Any special diets? The rest of the group eventually trickled into the building. It looked like they were filling out some kind of paperwork. At the center of the room was a table with a variety of foods. I was still nauseous from the migraine, but I knew I would be hungry later. My experience on the ship taught me to take food whenever it was offered because you didn't know when your next meal would be.

Now able to walk, I decided to pocket a couple of apples from the dining table before joining my parents who were filling out their paperwork. After filling out everything, we were directed to a row of chairs to sit in and wait for further instructions. We sat at the far end of the room away from the rest of the passengers. If anyone was infected, we didn't want to take the chance of getting the virus just as we had escaped the ship. Our only goal at that moment was to get to our rooms and get some rest. If any of us contracted the virus, we knew there would be little likelihood of us leaving quarantine. Despite our efforts to keep our distance, the room filled in with people, making it impossible not to have some kind of contact. When our number came up, they showed us to a small apartment where we would be staying for the remainder of our time in Georgia, which we were previously told would be at least fourteen days. An escort then handed us our room key cards and took us to the apartment complex.

Home Away from Home

The apartment complex seemed nice enough from the outside. These were enlisted men's quarters. When I showed pictures to my husband, he thought it looked like a decent enough place to stay. However, as soon as I passed through the door, I realized that there was nothing nice about this place, and it was in desperate need of repair. Full disclosure, I'm sure my physical and mental state at the time contributed to this reasoning.

I don't know where they got the apartment. I assume it was used as a soldier's barracks. Whatever it was used for, there was little upkeep. The inside was dilapidated. There was mold on the walls and other surfaces, and it smelled of mildew. It looked as though the whole building had been abandoned. My parents and I were on the bottom floor, and our rooms were in the same apartment; so at least we were not separated and could still see one another. Each apartment shared a kitchenette. There were no dishes, cups, or utensils, and the fridge was completely empty. There was a stackable washer and dryer, but no detergent. Luckily, I had brought my own, so my parents could do their laundry. Our apartment at least had electricity and running water, which we found out was apparently a luxury from those staying in other units.

I was glad that I had the prompting to bring my own detergent so we could wash our clothes while we were there. I also had kept some water bottles from the ship so we could fill them up and drink out of them. The extra shampoo would also come in handy since nothing was provided other than a bar of soap.

There was a shared bathroom, which was in equally bad condition. The bathtub had some sort of off-colored soap scum in the bottom of it. At least I hoped that was what it was. Grime and dirt surrounded the base of the toilet. They did provide towels by the sink, though I wasn't sure I would dare take a shower in that bathroom.

There were two bedrooms, one for me and another for my parents. The rooms were almost completely barren with the exception of the bed, a dresser with a TV on it, and a table with one chair. The condition of the rooms reflected the same lack of maintenance that the rest of the apartment had demonstrated. It was filthy and smelled of mold. There was a discolored window lighting the room. Faint rays of sunshine revealed the thick haze of dust that floated in the air. I could not believe that I had left the already difficult conditions aboard the ship only to end up in a place that was far worse. At that point, I wanted to be back on the ship. The ship was familiar and less like a prison cell.

Disheartened, I left my suitcase by the doorway of the bedroom and sat down to feel out the condition of the bed. It was stiff as a board. I pounded my fist on it with little give. You could literally bounce a ball off of it. Sleep would not be pleasant. Luckily, we brought our own pillows because I was certain the bedding was not properly washed. The first morning after we had slept there, my mom woke up with three or four red spots on her legs. We wondered if it was due to bedbugs. Needless to say, we decided not to take our pillows home. As horrific as the condition of the apartment was, it was the least of my worries. They could have put us up in a five-star hotel, and I would have still been dissatisfied. I wanted to be home.

The first day I was there, I ventured out to look for food. We hadn't had anything to eat for quite some time. The lady down the hall from us came out to greet me. She had a warm southern drawl and the sweetest voice. We talked for a few minutes. I told her about my mom's health and how I was looking for food for her. A concerned look crossed the woman's face. "Can I pray with you, dear?" she asked kindly.

We weren't from the same religion, but we both trusted in God. I agreed, and the woman placed her hand on my left arm and offered a heartfelt prayer on my behalf. She may have been a stranger, but she was a sister in faith. That prayer meant a lot to me. I could feel her faith as she pleaded for my mom's healing.

After saying the prayer, she removed her hand from my arm. "Oh my gosh," she exclaimed. "I'm so sorry. I shouldn't have touched your arm."

I smiled with teary eyes. "It's okay," I said. "I'm not worried about it. Thank you for your prayer." There was just something about the need for human touch to convey comfort. It came naturally and without thought. It was this quarantine that was unnatural.

The woman returned to her room, and I continued my search for food. I didn't find food, but I did find some personal-care kits containing hygiene products. I took a couple for my parents so they could at least have toothpaste and a few cleaning essentials. Continuing my search outside, I stepped into the open night air.

The guardsmen had constructed a chain link fence with black plastic around the entire complex. Large towering lights run by generators illuminated the area around the apartment buildings. Military police sat in their cars outside the fence, keeping an eye on us. There was no way we were getting out of here on our own accord.

Guarded quarantine compound

I tried to think of the guards outside as protectors, like the coast guard that protected the cruise ship while in the Oakland harbor. I'm not saying that wasn't the case, but somehow it was more difficult to believe, given our experience getting here and our treatment while in Georgia. Looking around my room, it definitely felt like I was a prisoner. I felt that I was being held against my will. I didn't do anything wrong. I wasn't sick. And yet I was confined in these horrible conditions, and I'm quite sure no one could've ever anticipated something like this happening around the world.

Passing the Days
Day ten in quarantine

Minutes seemed like hours staying in that small apartment. If I were actively doing something, I could at least pass the time faster, but all we did was wait. The stress of the ship experience and the constant worry of how long we would have to stay in Georgia did not help the situation. We had no idea when we would be able to go back home. We heard talk about fourteen-day quarantines, but we were under the impression that the quarantine would be at home—not in some apartment across the country—and wouldn't officially start until we were tested for COVID-19.

FaceTime with my husband helped pass the time. He was struggling with the circumstances as well. Mostly because he felt powerless to do anything to free me from my situation. When he had heard we were going to Dobbins, Georgia, he looked up the distance from home. It was exactly 1,967 miles from the doorstep of our house to the base where I was being quarantined. He felt this was a good omen since my birth year was 1967. I don't know that it was necessarily a good omen, but maybe it was just one of those little heavenly messages from God, saying, "Hey, don't worry. I'm here for you."

Mark continued to fight on our behalf to get us home but had very little success getting a straight answer from any government agency. It was as if I had committed some federal crime and was being incarcerated. There was no thought to the conditions we were in and no communication of what would be done with us.

As time passed in Georgia, I started to get the impression that things were not going to get better. The place looked like a prison camp rather than a quarantine facility. It was difficult to see it any other way. It didn't help that the migraines continued to plague me, which tended to mess with my mind. I floated between bouts of anger and outrage to melancholy and depression. I was physically exhausted and mentally broke. I didn't know how much more of this I could take. I know there are those who have suffered far worse. But I wasn't a soldier trained for hard things. I wasn't a martyr dying for a cause. I was just a suburban housewife wanting to go home to my family.

It's easy to discount the sufferings of others and make light of another's actions. The truth is, we have no idea what others are going through. Whether it's a chronic pain or an emotional scar that plagues an individual, we have no place to judge them. I thought myself both physically and emotionally healthy. I had been through hard things in my life. I knew plenty of my own suffering. But the culmination of what I experienced between the ship and that time in Georgia brought me to my breaking point many times.

What was surprising to me was how easily a person can break down when under those conditions. It put those stories of suffering into perspective. I had more appreciation for the courage of those that endured so much.

I always try to stay positive. I try to fight against negative thoughts. But all my best efforts were not enough. I often turned to God in the darker times. I know of no other way that I could have survived. I will forever be grateful for the strength He gave me in those weakest moments.

Other Concerns

As if the room and the treatment weren't bad enough, there were still more trials ahead.

"I'm sorry," the pharmacist said as we spoke over the phone. "We don't have any in stock for your mom."

"She was on a priority list," I exclaimed. "She needs medication. She is completely out."

"I'm sorry, ma'am. We can't do anything for you," she said.

"What do you mean you can't do anything?" I was angry, and my voice showed it. "My mom will die if she doesn't get her insulin. How can you say that there is nothing you can do?"

"We're out of stock," the woman said again—this time, gruffer.

I was incensed. Our biggest concern while in Georgia was getting medication for my mom. Her blood sugar was way too high. We had tried to get medication while on the ship but received nothing. When filling out the forms the first day, my mom put down that she needed medication due to her diabetes, but we had not heard whether they were going to get the medication to us. My mom rarely complained about anything, and since we had little contact on the ship while in quarantine, I couldn't see what the impact of having no medication had on my mom; but now that we were in the same apartment, I could see that her health was deteriorating.

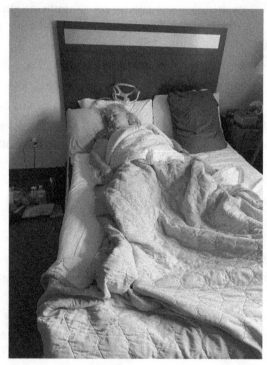

Mom not doing well

Most of the day, she laid on the bed, too tired to do anything. She was completely zapped of energy. My parents spent most of their time in bed. I think their bodies had been overwhelmed by the stress, and there really was little to do in the apartment and nowhere to sit.

"Is there someone else I can talk to?" I demanded.

"Ma'am, I have another phone call I need to take," the woman replied. The next noise on the line was the click of the receiver. She had hung up.

Frustrated, I threw my phone against the bed. It, of course, bounced.

A cousin of mine named Kate Davis that worked for the Department of Health in Salt Lake City, Utah, tried to help us. Over several conversations, she had managed to get my mom's medication and had it delivered to the tarmac at the Dulles Airport in Washington, DC, where we were supposed to be flying out of. But we still hadn't been released, and we had no means of getting the medication while stuck in quarantine. I had tried to talk to someone, anyone, in charge to see if we could get clearance to retrieve the medication, but no one would listen. We even contacted the governor of Utah to arrange something, but nothing was done.

A knock came at the door; they were delivering lunch. As I took the lunch from the volunteer, I told him of my mom's situation. "She's very ill," I said. "She has medication waiting for her at Dulles Airport if we can just go and pick it up."

"You're not allowed to leave," the volunteer said. "You have to be repatriated."

"But…"

"I'm sorry," he interrupted. "We will bring around medications tonight. I'm sure she will get her medications then." He turned and continued down the hall.

At the time, I had no idea what he meant by repatriated. I was on a cruise ship docked in Oakland. Apparently, to the US government, I might as well have come from a foreign country. I had no rights that I could voice. Those guards outside were not there to protect us; they were there to keep us from escaping. That's what it meant to be in a federal quarantine in what I had thought was my own country.

The evening came and went with no medication. I argued more with the attendant who brought dinner but received the same response. Medication was coming.

I went into my mom's room to check on her. She was lying on her side on the bed, nearly passed out with her insulin pen loosely gripped in her hand. She had tried to get the last drops of liquid out of it with no success. I took the pen from her hand. With soft, tired eyes, she glanced up at me. A slight smile crossed her face. Even in her weakened state, she was trying to console me with a smile. Tears welled in my eyes as I looked at her. I didn't have to say a thing; she knew the medication wasn't coming.

I returned to my room and laid on the bed in my empty room. Tears spilled out onto my pillow as I pleaded for my mom's life. I was angry, and I was tired. I felt helpless, wrongfully imprisoned for merely being in the vicinity of another person with a virus that neither of us had control of. Again, I prayed for God to deliver us from this place. I prayed for my mom. "Please don't take her from me," I begged. "Not like this."

With nothing else to do, my father turned to God as well. He decided to give my mother a blessing. When a person is sick as my mother was, the person giving the blessing anoints the head with special consecrated oil. My father performed such a blessing on my mother. My mother didn't miraculously get up and walk, but she did receive the assurance that she would need. God was with her and would provide a way for her.

He then gave me a blessing. I think he could see I was crashing physically and emotionally because of the constant headaches, the worry over my mother, and not being able to go home. As he placed his hands on my head and pronounced the blessing, I could feel God's love. There was a peace that came over me, and it became clear to me that He was there with me and had been there the whole time.

Throughout our trip, we had seen hearts everywhere. They showed up in the rocks on the beach and in the leaves on the trees. There were hearts in the scenery and even hearts in our dessert during our formal dining night. At first, it just seemed like a coincidence, but as they kept occurring, it became difficult to deny that there was some sign or omen there. I believe that those hearts were just some of the ways that God assured me that He was there. The feeling I received during that blessing from my father and the one I received from my husband on the ship were just a confirmation of this belief.

Since there was no one else around who could give my father a blessing, a church leader from home gave him a blessing though video call, just as Mark had done for me on the ship. Those blessings brought great comfort in a very difficult time. It helped remind us that God's hand was working in the background to get us safely home.

The next morning, my dad continued to call the pharmacists. They told us that they didn't have the insulin that my mom took, but they had regular insulin. We didn't know the difference, and we didn't know what it could do to my mom. My dad called my brother Burrell, who is a practicing pharmacist in Arizona, to see if it would be safe. My brother talked to the pharmacist who was delivering medications to others quarantined in our building and told him it would be okay to give her nine units of regular insulin.

Later that evening, the pharmacist and nurse came back and brought the insulin. My mom got out of bed and walked to the door where the nurse was standing, ready to test her glucose level. Her blood sugar was alarmingly high. She was experiencing hyperglycemia. Having too much sugar in her blood for long periods of time can cause serious health problems. It could damage the vessels that carry blood to her vital organs, increasing the risk of heart disease, stroke, kidney disease, vision problems, and nerve problems.

The nurse administered the insulin, injecting my mom in the stomach. She waited by her side to make sure she was okay. The injection seemed to be working. My mom rested as we continued to monitor her for further signs of insulin shock. She was going to pull through. I know that if it hadn't been for that shot of insulin, my mom would not have survived. It was a miracle that they had the insulin and a miracle that my brother happened to be a pharmacist who could suggest the right dosage. We will forever be in the debt of Commander Z and Jessica, two wonderful selfless volunteers on Dobbins Air Reserve Base.

That incident stayed with me. I knew God was with us and was going to see us through to the end of this ordeal. The next morning, I went to check in on my parents. They were doing much better. My mom's blood sugar had gone down to the low 200s. Normal is less than 140. Even my dad seemed in better spirits. My mom was able to sit up and walk around. And although she wasn't at her full strength, she was better than I had seen her in a while.

Returning to my room, I noticed a missed call on my phone. I called the number back. It was someone from the base. The man on the other end announced, "Everyone needs to be packed and outside the room by 10:00 a.m. You're going home."

CHAPTER 7

I'm Comin' Home

Sunday, March 15, 2020
Day eleven in quarantine and day twenty-four away from my family.

Outside the apartment complex, the bus arrived at 12:30 p.m. to take us to a small airstrip on the base. At the airstrip, the National Guard waited with a chartered SwiftAir cargo plane. There were thirty-one passengers, including us. Eight would be dropped off in Helena, Montana, and the rest would continue on to Salt Lake City. I only knew about the flight plan because my son Kenny was tracking the plane and had been texting me the route details. The National Guard did not give us any information about our destination until we were boarding the plane.

It was comforting to know that my family was keeping an eye on us back home. I know that it was the prayers and efforts of loved ones at home that made our release possible. I couldn't wait to see them again; it had been so long. This whole ordeal was taxing for all of us, and it seemed like I would never make it to this point.

As we entered the plane, each of us received a letter that read:

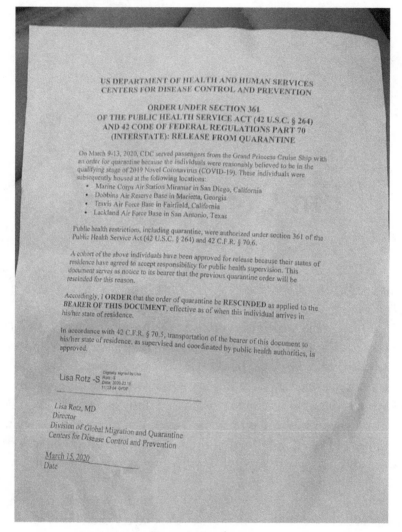

Repatriation letter

On March 9–13, 2020, CDC served passengers from the Grand Princess Cruise Ship with an order for quarantine because the individuals were reasonably believed to be in the qualifying stage of 2019 Novel Coronavirus (COVID-19).

A cohort of the above individuals have been approved for release because their states of residence have agreed to accept responsibility for public health supervision. This document serves as notice to its bearer that the previous quarantine will be rescinded for this reason.

Accordingly, I ORDER that the order of quarantine be RESCINDED as applied to the BEARER OF THIS DOCUMENT, effective as of when this individual arrives in his/her state of residence.

It was fitting that this whole ordeal started with a letter and would now end with one. The one letter had made me an exile to my nation. With this letter, I was now reinstated as a citizen with rights. The idea that my status as a citizen could change was strange to me. I was born and raised in the United States. I paid my taxes, voted in elections, and supported leaders, soldiers, and law enforcement. As a citizen, I enjoyed prosperity and freedom and the benefit of having my basic rights upheld by what I deemed was a fair and just system. I had never expected that a simple virus would strip me of all that.

Don't get me wrong. I'm happy to be back in full citizenship. It was just disconcerting to me that by no action of my own, I had become an exile to my own country and that it required this letter to give me an official status again. I know that COVID-19 has presented our nation with its share of tough dilemmas, but I have to question if these actions are really necessary and will not have repercussions later.

Homeward Bound

On the plane, I chatted with the flight attendant. She was a trauma surgeon from Hawaii who had volunteered to help the people on the plane along with the National Guard. We talked for quite a while during the flight. She was so kind to me. I suppose that after being treated like a prisoner while I was in Dobbins, it was refreshing to have someone treat me like an actual person. The entire flight crew was kind to us.

Our first stop was Montana. The landing was rough. The pilot came over the intercom and warned us to prepare for the landing. The plane shuttered and rattled as it came in for its approach. The wheels touched down with a large jolt that startled everyone. After everything we had been through, I don't know that anyone of us would be surprised if the plane crashed. Once the initial shock was over, the plane stabilized and came to a long halt. It was probably one of the scariest landings I have experienced.

Chili's cheeseburger

On the ground, the National Guard provided burgers and fries for us from Chili's. It had been such a long time since our last meal, and it was a relief to get good food. Most of what we ate at Dobbins was not much better than the things we were getting during those last days aboard the ship. The smell of the burger was like heaven. I generally don't eat meat, but I was so starved for a decent meal that I was happy to have a cheeseburger.

The treatment from the crew on that transport renewed my feeling of worth. Since the lockdown, our treatment had slowly deteriorated, causing great stress. Our treatment while at Dobbins did not alleviate any of that anxiety. The entire time I was there, I felt as though I had been cast off from society like some sort of untouchable without consideration for my rights as a human being. The flight team home, on the other hand, had made us feel like we were worth the sacrifices they were making. They showed genuine concern and kindness. Their actions made all the difference.

I realized that the efforts of those on the ship, at Dobbins, and on the flight were sacrifices. I'm sure none of them wanted to be in that situation. Somehow, the attendants on the ship and the plane did more than just help; they administered genuine aid. You could feel their intention was more than just doing a job. It was a sincere desire to make our situation more bearable by whatever means they had available to them, whether it was a kind word or going the extra mile to make sure we had what we needed.

One thing that this experience has taught me is to be considerate of how we serve people. There's a saying that "Beggars can't be choosers." That's true. We're all beggars at some point in our lives. While in lockdown, we needed a lot of help. We had no choice but to accept what was given to us. But how that assistance is given does have an effect on people. It affects how the receiver of that service sees themselves. When that service is given begrudgingly, the person feels like a burden that is being dealt with. But when service is done with kindness and love, the person feels like they have worth, that they matter.

Before the end of the flight, I gave my last heart card to the doctor and flight crew, expressing my deep appreciation to them and the sacrifices they made on my behalf. Elated, the nurse took the cards and showed the others. The crew stood at the front of the plane and placed their hands over their chest with their fingers curled into a heart shape.

One of them took the intercom and said, "Thank you for the card. It means so much to us. You have no idea how bad we needed to hear this today. We're so grateful for you and appreciate you." Everyone on the plane cheered and clapped with smiles and teary eyes.

What had been just a thought of gratitude for someone who had given so much had become words of support for otherwise weary servicemen, needing to feel appreciated. Just as fear, anger, hatred, depression, and selfishness can easily spread and harden hearts; charity, love, generosity, kindness, and gratitude can spread among open hearts, giving joy to all. It's our own choice how and what we decide to share. I found out later, they had framed the heart card and placed it on their supervisor's desk.

In Salt Lake

When we touched down at the Salt Lake City Airport, the crew escorted us to a hanger where we had our screening and debriefing. Medical personnel took us one by one and offered us a choice if we wanted to have the COVID-19 test or not. There were several people who chose not to have it done. I don't really understand this mentality; I wanted to know if I had it. My parents wanted to know if they had it.

They swabbed our noses so they could test us for COVID-19. The swabbing consisted of jamming a long Q-tip-like instrument up our noses. I had never had anything shoved that far up my nose. The sensation was not pleasant. It brought tears to my eyes and made me shiver all the way down my spine, causing me to do a sort of jig.

After the swabbing, we sat and waited for the rest of the group to finish. They had a box lunch from Jimmy John's, fruit, and vegetables on a table for us. We ate and awaited the rest of the instructions. While we waited, they handed each of us a thermometer.

Once everyone was seated, a medical team member talked to us about what we could expect for the next two weeks. "Your swabs will be sent for testing to verify that you are free of the virus. For the next fourteen days, you will be in quarantine in your home."

I wasn't too fond of the idea of being in quarantine again, but I was glad it would be at home and not in some government facility.

"You will not be allowed to leave your home," he continued. "During your time at home, you are to limit your time with others. That includes family members." He held up one of the thermometers. "You each have your own thermometer to measure your temperature twice a day while in quarantine and record it in the packet of papers you are given." After his announcements, he scanned the crowd and asked, "Are there any questions?"

Several hands raised, and for the next several minutes, he answered questions about the fourteen-day quarantine. What if they touched their luggage? Would it be contaminated? Was it safe to keep their pictures from the portrait packages taken while on the ship since they had been displayed and everyone could have touched them?

Some of the questions seemed unnecessary, but still they continued. By the time the discussion concluded, the sun had gone down. They took us to a waiting shuttle, and we were driven to a little parking lot just down from the National Guard section of the airport, where our family members were waiting for us. As we pulled into the lot, my heart leapt. I could see my husband in the distance wearing a black suit. My first thought was *Where did he even get the black suit?*

My husband was not a suit guy. He had an earpiece, shades, black ostrich-skin boots, and a skinny black tie. He looked like some sort of government agent from the *Men in Black* movie. He held up a sign that had been made by my kids and grandkids with "WELCOME HOME" scrawled in marker and cut out in paper. On one arm, he had leis for each of us, and tucked under the other were flowers.

Getting off the bus, I wanted to run toward him and hug him. I didn't care about social distancing; I just want to feel him next to me once more. In my mind, I could not believe I was finally home. I wouldn't believe it until I was in his arms.

First off the bus was my mom. She walked ahead of me toward Mark. He placed a lei around her neck, handed her flowers, and said, "Welcome home and thank you for having your daughter…" and then proceeded to scold her with tears in his eyes. He said, "Don't you ever do this again."

My dad walked ahead of me toward Mark. As he approached, my husband saluted him. My dad was a retired Air Force Staff Sergeant, and my husband always respected him for his service to the country. "Staff Sergeant, David George Richards," Mark's voice choked as he spoke. "Thank you for bringing my wife home. Job well done."

My dad smiled and saluted back. Mark placed a lei over his head and handed him flowers. Then he turned to me. He placed another lei around my neck and handed me a bouquet of flowers. Gerber daisies, my favorite. Tears were running down Mark's cheeks. My big strong man was always a tender teddy bear at heart.

We stood there for a long time not knowing what to do. I knew what I wanted to do, but I wasn't sure what I was allowed to do. "I want to hug you," I said. "I love you so much."

I looked at the health-care worker standing next to me. She had been watching our reunion. With a slight grin, she said, "I haven't heard that you can't hug him." She turned around as we embraced. I was finally home.

Tears ran heavy for all of us. Like a dream that I didn't want to wake up from, I refused to let go of him. With reluctance, I pulled away so we could pack our bags in the car. Mark stepped back and took his jacket off. "Now that the official welcome home is done," he said, "it's time for us to party." He pulled his white shirt off, revealing a bright red Hawaiian shirt, what he called his Magnum PI shirt.

"Now there's my husband," I exclaimed.

On the shuttle bus going to the airport going home

Mark saluting my dad

Home at Last

We drove to my parents' house first. While on the ship, Mark had informed me that the water main had broken to their house. I hesitated to tell them about it since they were already under enough stress in lockdown and there was nothing they could do about it. My husband gathered several bids, and the lowest was in the range of ten thousand dollars. I knew that my parents would be devastated. They really wouldn't want to spend that kind of money, and I didn't want them to go through a fourteen-day quarantine with no water.

When my husband's company heard what had happened, they offered to do all the work for the cost of materials. It was such an amazing offer. Mark was able to get the supplies for under one thousand dollars, and the company provided the labor and expertise. They had just finished fixing the main before my parents arrived. It was such an amazing relief for them and for me.

I know that it was providence from God that Mark received that job just four months before I left on the cruise. Because the basement to my parents' house had been flooded, Mark was able to clean it up before my parents even got home with the help of my children and their spouses and my siblings and their families. Although I missed him and would have liked to have him with me, if he had gone on the cruise, he would not have been home to ensure that my parents' home was taken care of.

I was extremely grateful to those workers who offered their time to fix my parents' water main. It was such an amazing act of charity. Many people offered their time, services, and resources to help us out. Their actions made our struggle so much easier. Later, my dad gave me a heartfelt letter of gratitude to give to the company, sharing his overwhelming appreciation for all those who had come out to work on the water main.

As ugly as these difficult situations can be, it's beautiful how they bring out the best in people. While I wouldn't want to go through it again, I'm glad to have experienced such kindness from so many. That isn't to say that there are not those who allow fear and anger to take control. There were plenty of those. Their actions made for trying times. But those individuals were outshined by the beautiful souls of those who stepped up to serve others. Their efforts brought peace in a relentless storm.

I had heard several stories of individuals who returned to their home, only to have threats against them by community members that disapproved of their home quarantine. Most of those stories were from the quarantined members of the cruise before us. Many were riled up into a terrified frenzy that COVID-19 might spread through their community due to all the media reports. Our community was not like that. They were more than generous with outpourings of charity toward our family.

I think by the time we got home, the strangeness and hype of the situation had died down. Many of them had already reached out to me on the cruise ship to see how I was doing, so they knew I wasn't sick. I was also extremely cautious when I got home. I didn't go out and walk around the neighborhood, at least not for the first few weeks. Although no one mentioned having issues with me walking about the neighborhood, I didn't want to make the situation any more concerning than it already was. I stayed home and obeyed the rules they had outlined in our debriefing at the airport. I wanted everyone to feel comfortable.

There was one rule that I did struggle with, and that was the rule that we should have limited contact with people in our household. Mark and I tried to adhere to it at first, but each day, we grew more relaxed. Eventually, we gave up on it altogether. I guess we felt that if one of us was going out with COVID-19, we might as well go together.

The Healing Process

When I walked through the front door of our house for the first time, I was overjoyed. Pausing at the entrance, I took in a heavy breath, pulling in all the familiar scents. I was home at last. My husband had made sure that everything was perfect. He even arranged the pillows on my side of the bed exactly the way I liked them. I'm a very particular sleeper. My husband calls me the Princess and the Pea. As I laid down on the bed, I felt it embrace my every curve. It was such a relaxing feeling after having slept on those hard mattresses in

Georgia. It was like floating on a cloud in heaven above. I have to say though the beds on the ship were surprisingly comfortable.

"You know," Mark said, "I kept it smooth and made sure that every pillow was in the proper place. It was sort of a ritual that I went through every night for the past three weeks." He sat down next to me. "I would lay awake every night looking over at that empty side of the bed, wondering if I'd ever see you back on that side of the bed." His voice choked as he spoke. "Now here you are."

I sat up and stared into his teary eyes. "I missed you so much," I said as we embraced.

The worries and concerns of the previous weeks just melted away. My body, exhausted and worn, now rested as my soul basked in the peace that surrounded me. I have been away from home many times and always returned with a degree of relief, but never had I felt so much joy to return home. It was more than just a soft bed and hot showers. It was family. It was Mark. It was the presence of those I held most dear. I imagine this is how our return to our heavenly home will be after this life.

That first night sleeping in my own bed felt wonderful. But my sleep was anything but sound. I woke up constantly in a panic, searching the room and wondering if I was on the ship or back at Dobbins Air Force Base. Sometimes I would relive the experience in nightmares. Each time, I would awaken with my heart pounding in agitation as the emotions flooded back. That continued for several weeks after returning home. Once I came to my senses again, I would realize that I was back home, which brought great relief. However, this relief was not enough to help me get back to sleep.

My migraine continued for several weeks after I came home. I spent much of the house quarantine in bed, mostly because of the migraines but also because I was not able to go outside. I knew I wasn't sick, but somehow my body didn't agree. I was tired and unmotivated. Maybe it was just exhaustion or depression brought on by the experience. When I did get out of bed, I would walk around the house, looking out the windows at a world I couldn't join. Being in bed was comforting though. I think the constant rest was just part of the healing process.

I wanted to go out and exercise, but I couldn't with the quarantine. I wanted life to go back to normal so bad. I wanted to go back to the pool and visit with my friends, but that couldn't happen anymore. I had exercise and yoga equipment, but even that was difficult to get motivated by with the migraines and the constant feeling of fatigue. I have a saying that "Motion is lotion." From my experience, if we aren't active and moving about, we begin to stiffen. When we're stiff, we have a more difficult time getting ourselves to move. It's like a perpetual cycle that is difficult to come back from. I had been so inactive while in quarantine that I was stiff.

It took great effort to do anything, so I began with something simple. I started with light stretching and sit-ups, any little thing I could to get my body moving. As I pushed myself to move, it became easier. The stress of the past several weeks had built up in my head and neck, contributing to my headaches. With the help of the stretching and exercise, the tension began to melt away, and with time, my migraines became more manageable. It was going to take time for me to get back to my active, energetic self, but these small daily efforts were at least a step in that direction.

The emotional stress was perhaps the most difficult to tackle. I constantly worried that I might get sick. I didn't feel any symptoms, but from what the media had said, the symptoms didn't always show up. So I waited nervously for my test results to come back. When the results came back three days later, they came with a caveat that exposure may have happened after the test was taken during the shuttle ride or on the airplane. While I was relieved that the test came back negative, the idea that I could still be infected was an ever-present reality. I would stay awake at night worrying about it, and I can't explain it. I didn't feel sick, but the possibility of having the virus would dwell in the back of my mind; and my body responded as such.

Meditation helped me process some of the feelings and worries that I was having at the time. It helped calm my mind while relaxing the tension in my body. I've always felt that there is a connection between our emotional well-being and our physical health. When we carry a lot of emotional trauma, it can manifest in weakness and even illness in the body. I've used meditation in the past as a means to alleviate that emotional strain, and it helped me heal after the events on the ship and at Dobbins.

A quote by a former leader of my church, Thomas S. Monson, has brought me great insight on how to work through the hardships I faced on the *Grand Princess*:

> *So much in life depends on our attitude. The way we choose to see things and respond to others makes all the difference. To do the best we can and then to choose to be happy about our circumstances, whatever they may be, can bring peace and contentment. We can't direct the wind, but we can adjust the sails. For maximum happiness, peace, and contentment, may we choose a positive attitude.*

I can't choose the difficulties I face in life. I can't protect myself from every danger. However, with the right attitude, I can live in a place of peace and contentment. I can choose to be happy despite my circumstances. The path to recovery won't be easy. It will be bumpy, and there will be times when I want to give up; but I will face it the same way I faced the challenges of the *Grand Princess*—with a grateful heart and a positive attitude.

My parents were also in their own recovery. My mom's health was not the same after the ship and quarantine facility. She spent many days in bed unable to function. She struggled to get her blood sugar under control despite medication and diet. Eventually, she did return to her normal levels, but the experience had taken its toll on her body. I didn't know how long it would be until her health returned or if it would at all. Despite physical exhaustion, my dad seemed to have fared better. He spent most of the home quarantine nursing my mom back to health, working around his house and helping my sister with a couple of projects.

When the last day of quarantine came, I walked out of my house into the open rays of the sun. The birds chirped their morning song while the breeze meandered past with the fragrance of morning dew. Friendly faces greeted me from afar with welcoming and encouraging smiles. The whole earth lay before me, blossoming with possibilities. Taking in a deep breath of a new day, I stepped outside and joined the world again.

CHAPTER 8

Moving Forward

I would like to say that by the time the quarantine ended, I was fully recovered. After all, I was sleeping better, my energy levels were recovering, and my migraines were becoming less frequent. But there were still aspects of my physical and emotional well-being that had not recovered. I don't think it's something that can heal overnight. It takes time. I still struggle to be around people. I guess it's a kind of post trauma from the experience.

I rarely leave the house, and I struggle to do daily things. If we need groceries, I will go with Mark, but I won't go in the store. I just wait in the car. Being on the ship and on the base has pro-grammed me this way, at least for now. We have gone up to our cabin in Wyoming with my parents and Quin and Susan. It's nice up there. Beautiful, serene, and secluded. I feel in my element there.

In June, the pool will open up again, and I will continue with my water aerobics. Maybe that will help bring back some degree of normalcy. I have slowly worked my way back to my old activities, my art, and my family. I reached out over social media to others from the *Grand Princess*. These are all part of my eventual healing. The events of COVID-19 have definitely left their mark on my parents and me. Time will tell whether it will be a lasting scar or a passing memory.

Writing this book started as a cathartic practice that helped me process the thoughts and emotions of the events. It allowed me to relive those events with a healthier perspective. Part of positivity is understanding that you won't be positive all the time. It's unrealistic.

Fear and anxiety will often overtake us, and we may act in ways that are negative, whether it's acting out in anger or allowing fear to direct our thoughts. By going back through the moments, you can accept your own frailties and make realizations that will help you face those same situations later in life.

Our lives are like classrooms where we go to learn principles of character and discover our ability to express love. We often fail and make mistakes, but that is part of the learning process if we allow it to be. By not hiding from our weaker selves but showing the same acceptance we would of a child who is just starting to walk, we can explore those aspects of ourselves and learn from our mistakes. On the other hand, pride and fear keep us from evaluating this side of ourselves, dooming us to an endless cycle of the same mistakes.

Returning to that time on the ship, I released a lot of emotions I didn't know I had. I could vent those feelings safely instead of acting them out in destructive ways. I could then let go of them and keep them from poisoning other aspects of my life. If my recording of these events have no greater benefit than that, it was worth it. I hope that by sharing my experiences, I can help others who may be going through similar experiences due to COVID-19 or any other difficult circumstance. Hopefully, I can help others look at the situation with a different and more helpful perspective. How we view a situation makes a big difference. It can totally change how we feel and react to the situation.

If I have one thing I can share about my experience, it's that despite all the hail and thunder and blustering winds, every storm has its rainbow that follows. It's often hard to see that end on the horizon; but it's there, and it's often closer than we think. If our head is weighed down by feelings of gloom and doom, if we turn away from the storm because of fear or anger, we will miss the breaking of the storm. We must look into the storm with our eyes heavenward to see the rainbow that follows. Only then can we see God's promises realized.

Don't dwell on the bad stuff in life; it will only pull you down and make you miss the blessing of heaven. It's okay to experience hard times and feel bad. Just don't unpack your bags and live there. Look to the good in the world, the love of God that dwells in the hearts of those that strive to hold on to the better part of their humanity. The COVID-19 pandemic and the events that follow it have been and will continue to be horrific for all those involved. It will change everything. I'm not trying to minimize the severity of this event by suggesting that we stay positive. On the contrary, it is because of the severity of the situation that we need to be positive. It's too easy to let the negative emotions overtake us in this huge maelstrom that we're facing. I'm trying to show through this book that how we react to the situation will have a lasting impact on ourselves and others. That impact can be positive.

I believe that my experience on the *Grand Princess* tested my resolve to be positive. The fact that I may have faltered during the trial matters little when compared to how I have left that situation. I've been tested and have come out the other side. Being positive to me is more than just a happy mantra; it's the way to a better life. I can say that because I've lived it.

Bridge the Divides

As people, our first thought in a tough situation is to lean toward the basic instinct of selfishness, fear, and anger. It's important that we don't become a victim. Instead, we should strive for something more. It takes a degree of restraint to stop our initial reaction and try to see things from a different perspective, especially when we feel we've been wronged.

It would have been easy in the heat of the moment to blame the cruise line and the attendants who were helping us. The natural tendency is to strike out against them, but those attendants had nothing to do with what happened. They were as much a victim of the situation as we were. It's easy to see every person in uniform as the enemy when we disagree with the government or those in authority. But if we're willing to stop for a minute and look at it from their perspective, we may find that many of those servicemen and women are sacrificing a lot on our behalf at a time when it would be very easy to only think of themselves.

I imagine the flight crew on our trip back home had escorted several people out of quarantine. Many of those passengers were likely not grateful and maybe even hostile. Those that were grateful may not have expressed it. To have someone, anyone, express appreciation for their efforts meant the world to them. Many people are like that—journeying through this world, doing the best they can, and not expecting anyone to recognize their efforts. When every good deed is invisible, how motivated will those people be to continue to sacrifice and serve others?

If we're to heal as individuals and as a nation, we need to reach out and be willing to listen to the other side. We need to be willing to see things from their perspective. Only then can we find a solution that will benefit everyone. Only then will we be able to get through this. I saw many times where small groups of people came together to help one another. The majority of people are willing to sacrifice for another out of a sense of compassion. People lose that compassion when they feel they are wronged or no one is listening to them. By reaching out, seeing the other side, and showing them that we appreciate them, we help them know that we care about them and their interests. Only then will they be willing to listen to us.

By working together, looking out for one another, and taking this pandemic seriously will we be able to control COVID-19. History has shown us that people who pull together can do remarkable things—overcome disease, endure the harsh realities of war, and maintain humanity in inhumane circumstances. Humanity has pulled through. There will always be something else out there looming over the horizon, waiting to strike, but we can tackle it. This is how humanity has survived for millennia: by working together.

Strive to Be Your Better Self

I believe we have it in ourselves to be better people. We don't have to give into natural tendencies of negativity. We can strive for something better, something higher, and something more positive.

I know it's easier to expect the world to change to our selfish desires. It's hard to turn away from the negative and seek out the good in us. It's not easy to forgive, serve, and sacrifice for others, especially those we feel have wronged us. But that is exactly what it means to be our better selves.

Someday, after all the lockdowns have ended and it's back to business as usual, you'll be on your way to work or to the grocery store and a driver will cut you off in traffic. Your initial reaction may be to yell at them and to disregard them as some kind of jerk. In that heated moment, I want you to stop...yourself—not the car, of course. Think about other reasons why they might have cut you off. Maybe they're rushing to get home to an injured child. Or maybe they're so distraught over losing a loved one and just didn't notice you. Maybe they're on their way to the hospital to have a baby. And maybe they are just a jerk.

All those scenarios are possible, but I would suggest that it's a rare occurrence that a person is just a jerk. No one is born a jerk. No one has lived the perfect life, and everyone has reasons to experience a bad day once in a while.

There are always layers of reasons why people act the way they do. People are just as messy as politics. The point is not to understand why they do what they do but to see the world as something more, something better. Because how you see the world affects your perception and your actions. You can choose to see it in a positive light or a negative. Those who choose to see it in a positive light are more willing to reach out to those who have otherwise been disregarded. They're the ones who are the bridge makers that bring people back together rather than dividing them.

There will come times when sacrifice is required. COVID-19 has shown us that. If we've practiced being our better selves in our daily lives—whether it's online, on the road, or in our home—we'll be prepared to step up. That is what I saw in those who served us. They did not hesitate. They knew that part of what made them who they are is their willingness to sacrifice when sacrifice was needed to help another. Their love and respect was an essential part of who they were. They were their better selves, and I am a better person for having met them.

I don't think we're expected to be selfless in the sense that our needs and wants don't matter. We don't need to nullify our existence for another's well-being. God doesn't expect unnecessary sacrifice. He just asks us to be our better selves. To treat others with the respect we would want. That's how we make a better world for everyone. That's how we pull together. Explore what makes you who you are. Just make sure you choose the better part of yourself.

The Path Ahead

Since quarantine, I've seen a lot of positive people. On social media, I've seen calls for a worldwide fast, including people from various faiths, and even those who are atheist but still understand the idea of solidarity. It has been an inspiration to me to see everyone pulling together. Obviously, there are still things in the world that threaten to divide us. Sometimes, it seems to be all the media focuses on. I'm not blind to the negative; I just choose to focus on the positive. Despite the fact that the more negative people tend to be the loudest, especially on social media, I've found that people have been positive for the most part.

Some that I've reached out to from the *Grand Princess* have had a lot of negative things to say about their time on the ship and in the various quarantine centers across the country, and rightly so. It was a bad situation all around. But despite the harshness of the circumstances that existed, the vast majority express overwhelming appreciation for all the volunteers that went above and beyond their duty to help us—nurses, doctors, servicemen and women, ship attendants, the captain. Words cannot express the gratitude that is felt for their efforts.

There are still plenty of concerns moving forward. The lockdown isn't over. Unemployment is at an all-time high. The economy may struggle to recover. Then there's the virus that still lingers out there. We were lucky enough not to get sick on the ship, but we could get infected from a grocery-store visit. Will my parents recover fully from the ordeal, or will there be continued complications? These are all very real scenarios, and yes, they do play out in my head.

When I find myself lingering on them and the fears and anger start to pull at my attention, I stop myself. In the end, they are just scenarios. I can try to anticipate them and plan for them, but I can't always stop them from coming. The most I can do is make the best decisions with what I have available to me at the time. In order to make the best decision, I can't allow my negative emotions to take charge. I have to push them aside and hope for the best. Only then can I see the best way forward. That is the power of positivity.

While I would not want to relive those events, I'm grateful for how they have proven to me that I can go through hard things and not be broken by them. My positivity and trust in God are what got me through, and it will get me through any other trials in life. I don't think I'm alone in that realization. This pandemic will prove many of us, and there will be many who come out the other side with that same trust. I believe the world will be a much better place when we leave lockdown, that the situation will have improved, and we will be better people. We may be more cautious about how we interact in public, but I believe people will be closer and will hug their loved ones a little longer. Love exists in great abundance in this world if we are only willing to see it. There is a shining spirit that unites us all because in the end, *we're all in this together.*

ABOUT THE AUTHOR

Monica knows how to work hard and to play hard. She loves Hawaii and is convinced she should have been born there, but instead was born in Ogden and raised by her single mother in Riverdale, Utah. It was on her eighth birthday her mother married David, who, soon after, adopted her and her younger sister and has been a wonderful father ever since. She has faithfully participated in water aerobics for years. When she's not near water, you might find her working on her parents' cabin that she and her family built from the ground up or maybe drawing a picture of the Savior with a special person. She always has a project that she's working on, and it usually involves helping someone. She is blessed to be a mother to six beautiful children and a grandmother to five amazing grandchildren. Monica married the love of her life and eternal companion (Mark) in June of 1985 when she was only seventeen years old. She feels blessed to call her husband of thirty-five years her best friend.

CPSIA information can be obtained
at www.ICGtesting.com
Printed in the USA
LVHW091147170521
687634LV00004B/56

9 781649 525048